Istanbul

● Ankara

TURKEY

Gazientiep →

Antalya
●

SYRIA

CYPRUS

LEBANON

A N E A N   S E A

YASMIN KHAN

RIPE
FIGS

Recipes and Stories from
Turkey, Greece, and Cyprus

Photography by Matt Russell

W. W. NORTON & COMPANY
Independent Publishers Since 1923

This is a book about food, of course. But it's also a book about love. And about loss.

It's a book about the recipes that travel with us on the great journeys our species have always taken, and how these recipes comfort us and nourish us through times of great celebration or terrible calamity.

It's a book about the people I met, shared meals with, and cooked alongside, in Greece, Turkey, and Cyprus.

But most of all, I think, it's a book about the resilience of the human spirit. And our capacity to endure the most unimaginable challenges and still find happiness in the smell of warm bread baking in an oven, a scoop of pistachio ice cream on a hot summer's day, or a bowl of roasted pumpkin soup eaten by a roaring fire.

And it's dedicated to all the migrants.

Refuge, Lesvos, Greece   11

Introduction   17
Borders, & other stories   27
The Greek, Turkish, & Cypriot pantry   29
Setting the table   32

Ripe figs, Athens, Greece   37

BREAKFAST   42
Honeybees, Athens, Greece   65

BREADS & GRAINS   70
Islands in the sea, Ikaria, Greece   91

MEZZE, LIGHT MEALS, & SIDES   96
Kitchen spirit, Lesvos, Greece   137

SALADS   144
Home for a day, Lesvos, Greece   171

SOUPS   180
To the city, Istanbul, Turkey   195

MAINS   204
The gypsy chef, Istanbul, Turkey   249

DESSERTS   256
A world without borders, Nicosia, Cyprus   283

Menu ideas   293
Dairy-free, gluten-free, & vegan recipe index   294
Index   296

Acknowledgments   302
Organizations to support   303

REFUGE
LESVOS, GREECE

The triumphant sound of Afrobeat blares from small, tinny speakers perched on top of the kitchen counter. The rhythm makes my head nod and my hips sway as I pick another tomato from the large pile in front of me, and use my paring knife to remove its hard white core. I throw this pith in the compost and slice the rest of the fruit into thick triangles before transferring them to a large plastic bowl with the rest of the tomatoes I've been chopping for the last twenty minutes. Next to me stands Sislo, my fellow line cook. Her head is down, repeating the same task, eyes focussed, hands quick. Reach. Slice. Toss. Compost. It's our moment of mindfulness for the day.

Earlier, Sislo told me that working here in the kitchen, at the One Happy Family community center, got her out of her head, out of her thoughts. Out of Moria, the largest of the official Greek camps on this island, where, at the time of my visit, 19,000 people live crammed into a space set up for 3,000. Or at least they did, until the camp burned down suddenly in the autumn of 2020. Out of Moria, where she doesn't feel safe. Where there are fights every night. Where you have to stand in line for hours and hours to get food handouts from the UNHCR and, at the end of that, sometimes when it's been handed to her she has opened it to find maggots inside. Food isn't always so perfect. Sislo misses the cuisine of her native Zimbabwe, she talks me through recipes for peanut stews and *sadza*. I glance at the pile of tomatoes in front of us and calculate that we have another hundred or so left to prep. A gust of Meltimi wind rattles into the makeshift kitchen hut from behind the open shutters. The island feels stormy today.

Tomato juice runs down my forearm, stinging as it meets a small graze on my skin. My eyes drift out of the window, where, across the ocean, I can just about make out the faint silhouette of Turkey. It's a stretch of blue sea that feels simultaneously beautiful and mournful, idyllic and haunted. I look away, take another tomato from the pile. Core. Slice. Chuck. Compost. I've slept so little since I arrived here, lying in bed night after night, my head spinning from the stories I hear, feeling angry and helpless at what

I am witnessing, guilty for the privilege of my passport, for the comfort I take for granted.

Suddenly there is a loud CLACK! CLACK! CLACK! behind me. I reflexively jump at the repetitive banging, turning to see the head of the kitchen, Mahmud, hammering at vegetables for today's lunch. A rat-tat-a-tat clanging rings from his chopping board as he finely slices a white cabbage, using the blade of his knife to scrape its shredded shards into a plastic vat. Once finished, he glances over at the large pot on top of the makeshift stove—two gas rings on which everything is cooked—and where at this very moment four or five pounds of onions are frying. "Mohammad!" he barks, eyeballing the chef who is measuring rice just ten feet away in this compact kitchen. Mahmud gives a sharp tilt of the head and gestures with his eyes, pointing to the cooking pot with the tip of his chin. Without a word, Mohammad sets down the rice and rushes over to the gas ring, stepping up onto a wooden crate so he can use the three-foot-long wooden paddle to stir the vegetables. The sweet, cloying smell of caramelizing onions begins to fill the air.

At 1 pm, the kitchen shutters open and three orderly lines form. First the children get served, then the women, then finally the men. Although, in my eyes, so many of the "men" still look so young, just boys. Such young boys. The pace and temperature of the kitchen pick up. I peer around the corner to check the lines and guess there are around six hundred people to feed today. Everyone has a task and we move quickly, aware this may be the only meal the people we are serving might eat today and that they are hungry. Pour. Scoop. Pack. Pass. Rice with a cabbage and tomato curry, seasoned with lots of cumin and coriander seed. The portions are small but densely packed and— most important of all—they are warm and nourishing.

A group of children approach the kitchen hut, straight out of this morning's math class. I watch as Sislo passes a bowl to a young Afghan girl. "Say thank you," instructs her teacher, who is next to the girl and her classmates. "Merci," says the little girl, shyly, and Sislo gives her a wide grin and a wink. The girl takes her lunch and heads to the collection of wooden benches and tables next to the kitchen, joining her classmates who are chattering in Dari as they look out to the shimmering Mediterranean. I hear the trill of her laughter as another gust of wind bounds over from the waves and whips us all in the face.

Introduction

For thousands of years, the Eastern Mediterranean has bridged cultures and continents through empire, trade, and migration. To think of the countries of Greece, Turkey, and Cyprus is to conjure up images of cobalt blue skies and shimmering seas, sun-drenched islands filled with olive groves and citrus trees, and mezze-laden tables filled with crisp rings of calamari and cigarillos of rice-stuffed vine leaves, all washed down with fiery anise spirits that make you cough and splutter. It's a place where family is central, tradition is honored, myths are revered, and meals are meant to be savored, slowly, and always with good company.

I first visited the Eastern Mediterranean more than thirty years ago, on a family vacation to the Western coast of Turkey. The trip is etched into my childhood memories, a last-minute deal booked on Teletext in what feels like another age, and which found us arriving twenty-four hours later in the hot and humid city of Izmir on the coast of the Aegean Sea. My parents, in typically spontaneous fashion, hadn't booked accommodation in advance, and so, through a mixture of expressive gesticulation, fluent Farsi and broken Arabic (the Turkish language has words from both), they soon befriended some locals. Before long we had a list of recommendations as long as our arms for hotels, restaurants, and sights we must not miss, and we set off to explore the expansive, stunning, turquoise coast.

It was, quite simply, one of the best vacations of my life. I felt like I had been initiated into a secret, parallel world filled with endless sunny days, seawater so soft and warm it felt like a bath, and a never-ending supply of all of my favorite foods. I spent my days feasting on sumac and lemon-doused fish kebabs, drinking cartons of piquant sour cherry juice, and picking up dense, sticky squares of pistachio baklava with my fingers, admiring them up close, all soft, glistening, and drenched in syrup. It felt a long way away from the gritty and industrial English city in the West Midlands where we lived.

I developed a particular affection for hot apple tea, fed to all the tourists, which was brought to me in an endless supply by shopkeepers as they tried to coax my parents into buying local hand-woven carpets. The result of at least one of those expert sales pitches still adorns my living room floor, its intricate patterns a happy reminder of that day.

This first trip to Turkey was an eye-opener for my whole family. We were moved—and, I think, comforted—by finding in the country a reflection of the warmth, hospitality, culture, and cuisine that we used to enjoy so much in Iran, but which, as a result of the political situation there, we could no longer easily access. I have made many trips to Turkey since, but that original vacation will stay engraved on my heart forever.

If my affection for the Eastern Mediterranean started as a child, it blossomed into a full-grown love affair by the time I reached my late twenties and moved to Northeast London, living just off Green Lanes in a house I've now called home for more than a decade.

Green Lanes is an area of London known for its long-settled Turkish, Greek, and Cypriot communities, a place where you can easily visit the Eastern Mediterranean every day through snippets of foreign-language conversations you hear on the streets, or via trips to the greengrocers. The fact that fig trees can be found in many of the gardens here is an added bonus. The aisles of my local shops are filled with crates of marinated olives, halloumi preserved in brine, and spicy beef *sujuk* sausages that call out to be thrown into a pan alongside a sunny fried egg. The shelves of these stores are laden with thin bottles of sticky grape molasses, small packages of gently hot *pul biber* chile pepper flakes, and jars of thick and creamy tahini, in both light and dark varieties. You'll often find me in the fruit and vegetable aisles, piling my basket high with pomegranates, quinces, sour green plums, and eggplants, as well as long green peppers and huge bunches of dill, parsley, mint, and cilantro that are sold at a fraction of the price you'd find in a supermarket.

My neighborhood carries a distinctively Mediterranean air about it, and yet it also is intrinsically Hackney, undoubtedly London. Specialty fishmongers line the main street selling red mullet from the Black Sea and sea bream from the Aegean. Turkish butchers, barbers, and bakeries, *lahmacun* and *pide* cafés, and baklava confectioners provide countless opportunities for tasty late-night snacks after an evening's adventure. On summer nights, I love to walk through the neighborhood inhaling the aroma of grilled meats that wafts out of the dozens of *ocakbaşı* kebab houses, where juicy cuts of lamb and chicken are barbecued over hot coals and served alongside fresh salads doused in turnip pickle and pomegranate molasses, or wrapped in charred flatbreads that have been smothered in meat dripping. I don't have to travel far to find the Eastern Mediterranean. It's right here, just a few steps away from my London kitchen. In today's globalized world, finding these pockets of different migrant communities in major cities is commonplace. It's one of the many benefits of migration; that wonderful exchange of labor, commodities, and cultures that has enriched so many aspects of our lives, including our kitchen cupboards.

For as long as humans have existed, we have traveled. First as tribes,

journeying in nomadic groups to provide resources for our community. Then as explorers, conquerors, traders, or missionaries seeking to engage, influence, or control others on this planet. More recently, we have started moving for pleasure, for recreation, for vacations. But one form of travel has stayed constant throughout time: the travel necessary for our protection and safety.

Many members of my family and our family friends have undertaken such journeys, fleeing political, economic, and social turmoil in the countries of their birth. Some won visa lotteries, others embarked on foreign study, a few were able to claim asylum, others still paid illicit smugglers to take them clandestinely over the mountains of Turkey so they could find refuge in Europe. Many weren't as fortunate; they couldn't escape when they needed to, and faced a life of limited opportunities at best, or imprisonment, torture, and execution for their political beliefs at worst. My childhood memories are littered with images of my parents' house in Birmingham filled with recent refugees from Iran, who stayed up late, smoking cigarettes and drinking endless cups of tea as they debated the region's politics. I'd find the remnants of those evenings scattered throughout the living room the next day: small empty clear glasses, with dregs of tea leaves at the bottom, along with crumbs from the torkmeh—toasted and salted sunflower, melon, and pumpkin seeds— that Iranians eat by the pound.

For all migrants, being uprooted from one's homeland is an unsettling experience, and as such people often become attached to things that help them to maintain a sense of identity. Language, religion, music, and storytelling all form part of a migrant's cultural toolbox, but perhaps nothing provides more of a sense of identity than food. The dishes my parents cooked when I was a child comforted as much as they nourished. Their recipes provided answers to the questions of where we were from and what values we held close to us. They told the story of my ancestors, who traveled from Kashmir to Punjab, from Gilan to London and California, and grew fields of rice, and pickled bulbs of garlic, and simmered quince in cardamom and rose water to eat for breakfast with toasted bread and clotted cream.

In recent years, as countries around the world have increasingly framed the movement of certain people as problematic, imposed travel bans against particular nationalities, and closed borders in the name of so-called "security" (often aimed at keeping out people who come from the countries of my ancestors), I realized, with much sadness, that to me these debates weren't just abstract, but an everyday reality, directly affecting me and my loved ones.

And so it was that as I watched, with increasing horror, the refugee crisis unfold in the Eastern Mediterranean in recent years, I started wondering about the stories of the migrants who were traveling through the region, and what borders mean in a globalized world. At the time of writing, an estimated five million refugees have come through Turkey, Greece, and Cyprus in the last five years—the biggest movement of people that Europe has seen since the Second World War. This is a huge number by any standards, but perhaps just the tip of the iceberg in terms of the kind of migration our planet might see as the climate and financial crises escalate, or if we face another health pandemic. Migration, and how we deal with it, is one of the key issues of our times.

The Eastern Mediterranean is in some ways a microcosm of this issue, encapsulating in miniature the challenges that many countries around the world are now facing. How, in the twenty-first century, do we deal with the fact that humans have always needed to move and always will move? And how can we update our narrative and our concepts of borders, states, and identity so that people can live, and move, in peace and dignity?

So I set out on a mission, to see what I could learn from traveling through Greece, Turkey, and Cyprus, eating, drinking, and cooking with people from all walks of life. What follows in these pages are recipes and stories inspired by my travels. It's a journey through clay-red soils, air that carries the fragrance of orange blossom and thyme, and hundreds of conversations over small cups of dense and sweet black coffee.

While the recipes in this book are inspired by the experiences I had and the people I met, they are all my own, and were created in a London kitchen using modern, accessible techniques. The stories reflect my understanding of a crisis that is unfolding and that we simply can't ignore. It is my hope that this book and the recipes within it will start a conversation about these important issues and—as far as I'm concerned—there is no better place to talk than at the dinner table.

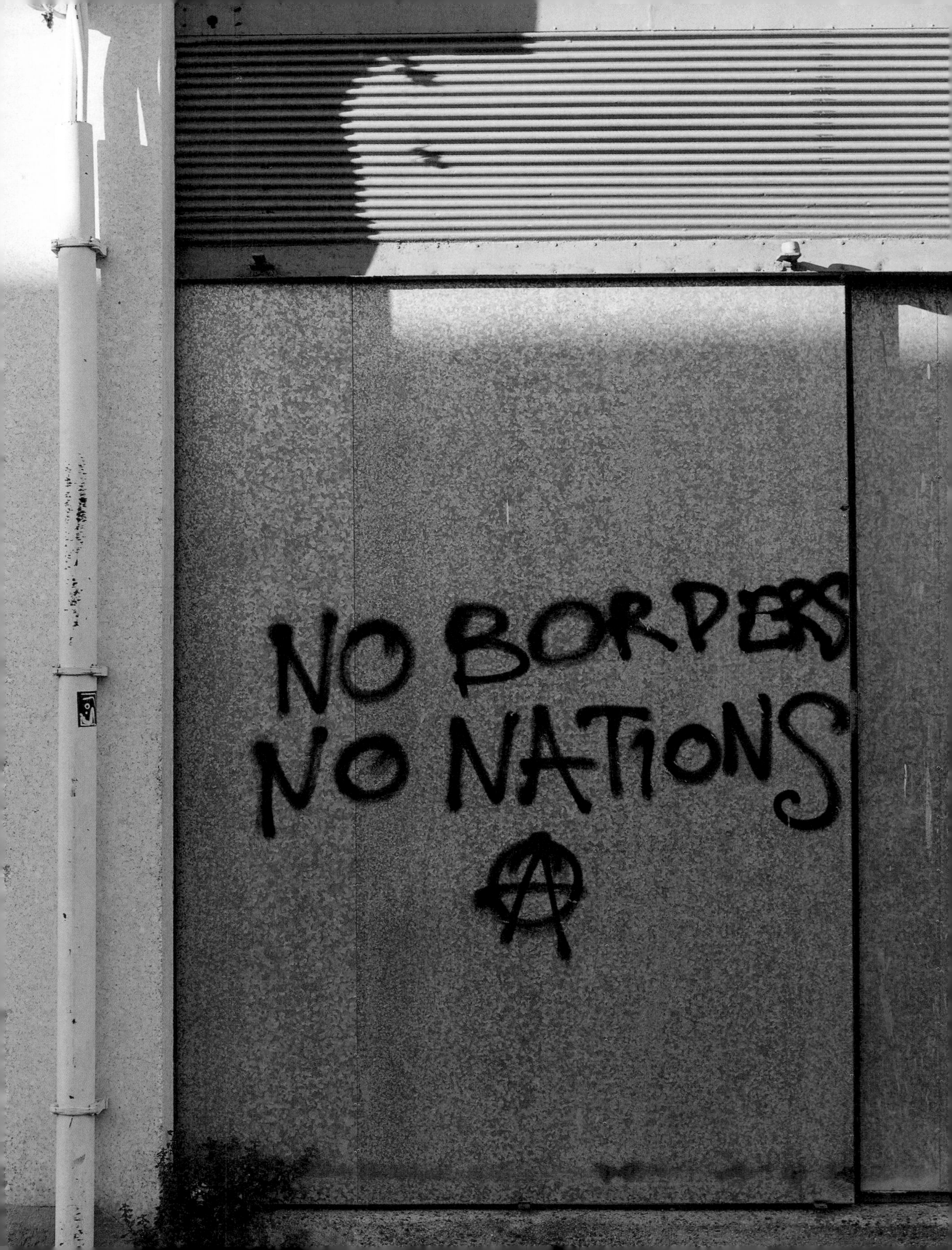
NO BORDERS
NO NATIONS

Borders, & other stories

The "Eastern Mediterranean" is a fluid term used to describe countries that are close to, or border, the East of the Mediterranean Sea. It is also sometimes used to describe countries of the Levant or parts of Northeast Africa and, as such, encompasses countries that are European, Middle Eastern, and African. For the purposes of this book, when I describe the Eastern Mediterranean, I'm primarily talking about Greece, Turkey, and Cyprus and the broad culture that unites those three countries, even though I am acutely aware that the term has much broader parameters too.

For thousands of years, the borders of the Eastern Mediterranean have been as contested as they have been fluid, with various empires occupying the land and colonizing the people who lived there. This has resulted in the countries of Greece, Turkey, and Cyprus sharing many similar cultural and culinary traits born not only out of proximity with each other, but also from similarities in climate and landscape and more than a millennium of ever-changing borders.

Both Greece and Turkey are relatively new countries in their current geographical constructs. The Republic of Turkey was created in 1923 after the fall of the Ottoman Empire, while Greece, in its current formation, gained independence from the Ottomans in 1821 and established its republic then.

Cyprus has a more complicated recent political history. After the fall of the Ottomans, the British took over the island and continued to rule it until the Republic of Cyprus was established in 1960, throwing off one of the last bastions of the British Empire. During British rule, tensions between Greek and Turkish Cypriots were fomented and exacerbated by the British ruling elites and—for students of colonial history—a frustratingly familiar story followed. After the British left, ethnic tensions continued to rumble, erupting in the early 1970s and culminating in a civil war that led to the island being divided in 1974. This division continues to this day through a United Nations-maintained buffer zone, known as the Green Line, which cuts through the capital, Nicosia, and separates the island into the Southern region of the Republic of Cyprus (predominantly inhabited by Greek Cypriots) and the Northern area known as the Turkish Republic of Northern Cyprus (mostly inhabited by Turkish Cypriots). Many of the Cypriots I have spoken to believe the division to be a constructed political fallacy, and so, for the purposes of this book, when I write of Cyprus, I am referring to it as one country, even though technically its borders separate it into two.

| SULTANBACI HALVA FISTIKLI £2.49 | SULTANBACI HALVA £1.99 | SULTANBACI HALVA £1.99 | AYTAC CACOA HALVA £1.79 | AYTAC SADE HALVA £1.79 | | KOSKA TAHIN £2.79 | KOSKA UZUM PEKMEZ £2.79 |

| ELIN OLIVE OIL 1lt £6.49 | SALAD OLIVE OIL £1.99 0.5lt | SABROSA OLIVE OIL £7.49 1lt | ULKER BIZIM £1.99 | SAFYA OIL 1LT £1.49 |

| EDA BEANS | DURU BULGUR 1kg £1.69 | DURU KOFTELIK BULGUR 1kg £1.69 | EDA BALDO RICE £1.89 |

The Greek, Turkish, & Cypriot pantry

If the regional border politics can leave you confused, it is strikingly easy to understand the food culture of Greece, Turkey, and Cyprus. I like to describe it as seasonal, abundant, plant-focused, and communal.

Each place, of course, has its many local and regional specialties, specific cultural contexts, and uses for distinct herbs and spices. And being plant-focused doesn't mean that meat isn't a celebrated part of the diet—far from it!—but rather that the plethora of vegetable dishes on the table have often been given just as much attention and care as the meat. Whole books have been written about the intricacies of each cuisine and—given how rich each place is in culinary culture—many more could be written. But, in this book, I'm pulling back to explore the regional *similarities*, of which there are many, especially around the ingredients used.

The Mediterranean sunshine and rich red soil produce a glut of fresh fruits and vegetables that, along with pulses and legumes, form the bedrock of food in the region. Add on to this excellent olives and olive oil, aged sheep and goat cheeses, thick plain yogurts, wild greens, fresh nuts, fragrant herbs, and a particular affinity for barbecued meat grilled over hot coals, and you can begin to see similarities where political borders insist upon division and difference.

The kitchen shelves of Greece, Turkey, and Cyprus share many common ingredients and are easy to replicate. You'll find large metal tins of extra-virgin olive oil, glass bottles of red and white grape vinegars, jars filled with dried pulses such as chickpeas, white beans, and brown lentils, and plenty of white rice, orzo pasta, and bulgur wheat. You can find these staples in most ordinary supermarkets or grocery stores, but there are a few key ingredients that I suggest you seek out in order to get the most from the recipes in this book.

OLIVE OIL

The quintessential Mediterranean ingredient and one that I recommend you invest in. Many of the dishes of the Eastern Mediterranean are subtly flavored, so often it is the quality of the oil that will make or break a dish. I have three bottles on hand at home. A full-flavored, high-quality, extra-virgin olive oil that I just use for dressings and final flourishes (and never bring near any heat), a medium-quality extra-virgin oil that I add to soups, beans, and stews while they cook, and a light olive oil that I use for sautéing and baking (though I almost always use a natural, neutral vegetable oil such as sunflower or canola for basic tasks like frying onions). It may sound like an effort to have all these bottles around, but it actually makes it more economical; you don't want to waste your fancy oil by cooking with it! Just remember that olive oil is very sensitive to heat and light, which will both make it turn rancid sooner, so store your bottles in a cupboard away from the side of the stove or any bright lights.

YOGURT, BUTTER, CHEESE, AND CREAM

If there is one category of food in which the Eastern Mediterranean excels, it's dairy. In Turkey, copious amounts of butter, cheese, and yogurt are consumed throughout the country, and they eat magnificent hot yogurt soups as well as the addictively salty and refreshing yogurt drink called *Ayran* (see page 106). Greece's thick strained yogurt is of such a high quality that it has become world renowned and, in Cyprus, you'll often find a bowl of tangy plain yogurt served alongside savory dishes such as stuffed vegetables or grape leaf dolma. When sourcing yogurts for the dishes in this book, try to buy full-fat and plain varieties. I stand firmly by the saying that what you lose in fat, you lose in taste.

The most famous dairy product of the region is of course the iconic white brined cheese known as *feta* in Greece and *beyaz peynir* in Turkey, which adorns salads and sandwiches, mezze platters, and breakfast spreads. When this kind of cheese is exposed to air, it tends to dry out and spoil very quickly, so to make your block of feta last longer, I highly recommend storing it in a salt water brine. Simply take 2 cups/500ml water and stir in 1½ teaspoons salt until the salt dissolves. Then place the block of cheese in it and stick it in a sealed container in the refrigerator.

Other popular cheeses in the region include halloumi, which, while most commonly associated with Cyprus, is actually eaten throughout the Eastern Mediterranean. Try and look for varieties made from sheep and goat milk (as opposed to cow milk) for an authentic flavor.

The dairy product you might have the hardest time sourcing—but which I have no doubt will bring you the greatest pleasure—is *kaymak*, a thick, luscious cream made from buffalo milk which has some affinity with clotted cream or mascarpone. It is hugely popular in Turkey (as well as the Balkans, Iran, Iraq, and Afghanistan) where there are whole shops devoted to *kaymak* production. Today it is mainly consumed for breakfast with honey and bread, though it is also served alongside baklava, or used to stuff pastries and pancakes. Clotted cream works as a useful substitute, but you can find *kaymak* in Mediterranean stores and I recommend you seek it out. If you look for it in an Iranian store, it will be labeled *sar sheer.*

DRIED HERBS

The pantry staples for the recipes in this book are thyme, oregano, spearmint, and dill. If you can, try to seek out Eastern Mediterranean varieties of these and you'll be rewarded with profound, multi-layered depths of aroma. Spearmint can be found in any Middle Eastern or Mediterranean store and is the one ingredient from the region I would love to see people in the West using more; it can't really be substituted with fresh mint as it has a completely different impact on dishes, so do try to source some if a recipe calls for it and let me know what you think!

DRIED SPICES

Cumin, coriander seeds, cinnamon, paprika, and nutmeg are the spices most commonly found in the dishes of Greece, Turkey, and Cyprus and it's likely you already have them in your pantry. What you might want to add is *pul biber* chile pepper flakes (also known as Aleppo pepper). These have a moderate heat with a fruity, tangy flavor and are used both in cooking and as a condiment in Turkey and Northern Cyprus, where you'll find little pots on the table alongside the salt and pepper.

Pul biber can be found in most supermarkets these days, in any Mediterranean store and, of course, online. Another essential Turkish spice to stock up on is sumac, a brightly astringent red berry that is crushed into a fine powder and used in kebabs, salads, and stews. I use sumac any time I want to add sour flavors to a dish.

FRUIT MOLASSES

The sweet-and-sour syrup of pomegranate molasses is often used in the cooking of the Eastern Mediterranean and a bottle can go a long way; I use it in everything from salad dressings, to stews, to cakes. Be sure to check the label when you are buying it to make sure there isn't any added sugar or—worse—added sweetener. I think it massively affects the taste (and not in a good way) and, anyway, it's better for the cook to be able to control the sweetness of a dish.

Grape molasses is another popular dark, sticky syrup that has been eaten for centuries throughout the region and has a uniquely rich, deep, and sweet taste as well as being renowned for its healthful and healing properties. It can be a little tricky to track down outside specialty Middle Eastern or Mediterranean stores, so I've mostly suggested using date syrup in the recipes in this book instead. If, however, you can find some, I highly recommend eating it as part of a Turkish breakfast alongside some bread and tahini or walnuts.

NUTS AND SEEDS

The Eastern Mediterranean climate and soil are perfect for walnut, pistachio, and hazelnut trees, so it's no surprise that these feature heavily in both savory and sweet dishes throughout the region. Nuts are sprinkled over yogurt for breakfast, ground into soups for lunch, layered into flaky pastries to enjoy with afternoon tea, and chopped into kebabs for dinner. I always have jars of these nuts on hand, but tend to buy them in small batches as they spoil quickly. It's incredibly important to keep them in airtight containers, or I sometimes freeze them if I know I won't use them immediately, as it keeps them fresh; they defrost very quickly.

Sesame seeds are also often used, especially in baking, but it's their thick paste known as tahini that you'll find most often on Eastern Mediterranean tables. Brands of tahini vary enormously and the quality of the paste you use can make such a difference to your cooking. I personally prefer to buy tahini paste from the Levant, as I think it tends to have the best consistency and flavor, so I always recommend sourcing Lebanese brands if you can.

Setting the table

One of the hallmarks of Eastern Mediterranean cuisine is that there are certain staples that always accompany a meal, no matter what you are eating. There will always be a fresh salad, some bread, olives, a few wedges of raw onion, and perhaps some pickles or chiles depending on what you are serving. If you are in Cyprus or Turkey, there will probably be a bowl of thick plain yogurt. A bottle of extra-virgin olive oil is also absolutely essential so that people can add it, as a seasoning and accompaniment (in my house, when we eat the dishes from this book, we always drizzle a liberal amount of olive oil over our plates just before eating). Salt and pepper are common seasonings, but *pul biber* chile flakes and some cut up pieces of lemon are also often present, so diners can adjust their plates to their personal preference for heat and sourness.

Presenting food in this way means that even a simple bean stew becomes elevated to an exceptional feast, so my one request when you are eating from this book is to include several of these staples with most dishes that you serve.

The other essential element to embrace about the Eastern Mediterranean way of eating is not to plate up food individually, but to bring all the dishes to the table and place them in the middle, so people can help themselves to as much as they want. And if you want to really adopt the Eastern Mediterranean culture, you would then keep insisting that people take more helpings than they want or need and continue piling food on their plates until they throw their hands up in protest. Up to you.

A final component that I think is important: let go of concepts about what type of food should be eaten at what time of day. In Turkey, for instance, it's not unusual to have lentil soup for breakfast, eat dessert in the middle of the afternoon, and enjoy eggs for dinner. Stepping away from a Western idea of what each meal of the day should look like will help you to enjoy these recipes more. And, for the record, dal and rice is one of my favorite breakfasts . . . but that's just me.

RIPE FIGS
ATHENS, GREECE

I wake early, as I do most mornings on this trip, make a cup of tea, and grab a pint of purple figs from the refrigerator. I head straight to the balcony, notepad and pen in hand, ready to sketch out the thoughts that come to me in these quiet first hours of the day.

The balcony is small. Too small to be comfortable if truth be told, with just enough space to fit a round table, two metal chairs and a few dusty succulents. But still. It catches the morning sun and, from high up on the sixth floor of an apartment building, it has a view looking out on to the Exarcheia neighborhood of Athens.

I pick a fig from the table—I bought them yesterday at the farmer's market down the street—and roll it gently between my thumb and forefinger, before bringing it to my nose for a quick sniff. I often smell food before I taste it, a quirk I used to think was a bit odd but which I now take as a representation of true enjoyment. When I want to appreciate something fully, I like to inhale it with all of my senses. It smells of damp wood and warm treacle.

A ripe fig needs careful handling. Its soft, waxy skin encases a tender heart that is easily bruised. I peel back its taut casing, stripping dark ribbons from stem to base, as I stare out at the city at dawn. My eyes fall, one by one, on sand-colored apartment blocks, crumbling walls, balconies covered with sun-bleached awnings, clothes drying on washing lines, graffiti-scrawled anarchist messages everywhere. I look down at the fig, completely naked now and a little vulnerable in my hands. I take a bite and the sweetness of honey fills my mouth.

It's my first time in Exarcheia, a neighborhood where Greece's intellectual left has historically thrived and which is notorious for its anti-authoritarian movements. In recent years, as the refugee crisis unfolded in the Eastern Mediterranean, the neighborhood's squats, social centers and radical cafés opened their doors to migrants without papers, offering them a space in which they could seek refuge and live with dignity away from the horrors of the official refugee camps.

It made sense to come here first, to start my journey exploring borders in this very ancient city facing a new version of a timeless question. Namely, what to do when millions of people turn up in your country and ask if they can stay, have shelter, work? How do we co-exist in a world where artificial borders are now more rigid than ever?

These lofty questions were at the forefront of my mind as I planned this trip, making long lists of all the people I'd like to interview; from anarchist co-operatives, to civil society groups, to those running refugee kitchens . . . and, of course, new migrants to the city. I envisaged showcasing this unusual neighborhood as a beacon of social solidarity in a broken global system, an example of alternative ways of being, sharing, existing.

But five days in and the task I had set myself feels Herculean, requiring strength I don't think I have. I sigh as I reach for another fig and begin the process of wearily peeling it again. No, not this trip, not this time. My biggest priority, as I sit on the balcony each morning, is simply to find the inner resolve to hold myself together.

There's this peculiar trait, I think, in modern travel writing. An imperative to write about your travels as if you are always living your best life. As if every experience is *amazing, incredible, upbeat,* as you pose to document smiles, meals, and a checklist of tourist attractions for your social media accounts. "Look at this beautiful view!" we post. As if the beauty that we have captured through our camera lens somehow reflects the beauty we want people to see within us. But here's the thing. Not all travel is like that. Not all travel is enjoyable. Some things travel with us, even if we'd rather they didn't. Sometimes, even in the most perfect setting, it's hard to see the beauty all around you and all you want to do is stay in bed all day. So, I might as well be honest, though you've probably guessed it by now: I was having a rough time in Athens.

It wasn't her fault. Athens is a majestic city, and I can see that clearly now. A punk spirit wrapped in an ancient democracy, home to people who are warm and generous with that wonderfully Mediterranean and Middle Eastern characteristic of being both extremely passionate and admirably laid back; it's a fantastic combination. There is so much to love about Athens and I know that. I wish I could tell her, "It's not you, it's me."

But, on this trip, I walk the streets of Athens with large sunglasses on my face to hide the bags under my eyes. Carrying a throbbing in my temples and a tightness in my chest. My steps feel heavy and cumbersome, as if gravity is pressing me down to the extent that the mere act of walking—normally my favorite activity as soon as I hit a new city—has become so arduous that

ΦΙΣΤΙΚΙ
ΧΛΩΡΟ
€:8.80

I could easily crawl up on a corner of the pavement and sleep there for a century. The traffic-clogged streets make my head spin. I taste nothing in the food and my body confuses me by feeling both completely numb and yet heightened with sensitivity at the same time. In retrospect, I probably shouldn't have embarked on a research trip to write a book about a complex and emotive issue just two weeks after a miscarriage.

With the benefit of hindsight, I know now what I didn't know back then, that the first few weeks following a miscarriage are as messy as they are disorientating, with hormone crashes confusing your body and your psyche oscillating between emotions as it adjusts to a new reality. A whole catalogue of emotions relating to your body is released that you didn't even know existed: Grief, Uncertainty, Anxiety, Failure, Fear, Anger, Shame. So yes, in retrospect, perhaps it wasn't the wisest thing to arrive in an unfamiliar city and attempt to reach out to strangers, day after day, trying to be cheery and convince them to meet me. Everything just left me numb.

I wake each morning at a loss about what to do, knowing that all I want is to sleep, wracked with the additional guilt that, compared to the many challenges of the people I am meeting, mine feels like a more fortunate position. But still, I am in Athens. There must be something that will help.

I reach for another fig and take solace in its sweetness. A ripe fig always reminds me of Iran, of my grandparents' farm, of the fig tree on the dirt path that led to their house, of hot summer days with my cousins running around the farm and picking fruit from the trees when we wanted a snack, of my grandmother's sharp eyes which always could spot exactly when a particular fruit was ready to be harvested. Sometimes, when you are in an unfamiliar place, living through a difficult and painful experience, food can comfort and nourish you in a way that few other things can. They say that food shouldn't be emotional, but how can it not be, so full of memories as it is?

So I sit on this balcony, morning after morning, eating as many figs as I can. Because ripe figs remind me of my childhood, of my home, of my community, of being loved. Ripe figs remind me of feeling safe.

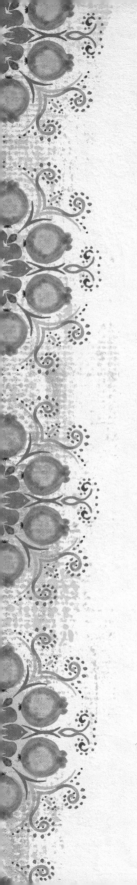

BREAKFAST

I crave solitude in the mornings and one of my favorite things to do is to get up very early to steal some quiet time to myself, before those around me have woken up. On my first trip to Cyprus, I spent a week in Plomari, a little village on the South of the island, in a tiny bungalow with a small but dense Mediterranean garden. The front yard was filled with walnut, citrus, fig, and pomegranate trees, their branches heavily laden with fruit. Each morning I'd get up at dawn, head into the garden with a shallow bowl and gently twist the purple fruits off the branches of the burgeoning fig tree. It became a daily ritual, taking on a meditative quality, as I gently squeezed the fruits between my thumb and forefinger to check for ripeness, then took them over to the picnic table under a canopy of grape leaves, where I would eat them for breakfast while they were still warm from the sun. It was there I decided that my highest aspiration in life was to have a home with a blossoming fig tree in the garden. Ripe figs for breakfast are honestly all I need.

Breakfasts in the Eastern Mediterranean can be varied, if truth be told. The Greeks traditionally eat quite lightly and are likely to have something simple and on the go: a pastry, a slice of cake, some bread and jam, or more often than not just coffee and a cigarette. Turks, on the other hand, are known to go all-out with the infamous Turkish breakfast, often served as an all-day brunch on weekends. These lavish morning feasts feature eggs muddled with tomatoes, several varieties of sheep, cow and goat cheeses, black olives, sweet tomatoes, crunchy cucumbers, a selection of jams (sour cherry and carrot are my favorites), *kaymak* (a type of clotted cream) alongside a slab of honeycomb, plenty of fresh fruits, and endless cups of tea. The Cypriots, as befits their mixed cultures, breakfast somewhere in the middle.

This chapter features a selection of recipes that cover the broad brush of Eastern Mediterranean breakfasts and that I have no doubt will—at the very least—give you a sunny start to your day.

Griddled fruits, yogurt, & honey

This is less of a recipe and more of a suggestion about how you might want to start the morning on a hot summer's day. Griddling the fruits isn't essential (you can bake them if you don't have a griddle pan), but it does help to soften and sweeten any that are not as ripe as you'd like, which is all too common in my part of world. Use thick, full-fat Greek-style yogurt and floral honey.

8 ripe figs, halved
6 apricots or plums, halved
   and pitted
3 nectarines or peaches,
   quartered and pitted
¼ teaspoon ground cinnamon
¼ cup/60ml orange juice
mounded 2 cups/600g strained
   full-fat Greek-style yogurt
handful of grapes, halved
handful of nuts, such as walnuts,
   almonds, and pistachios,
   roughly chopped
½ cup/170g honey

SERVES 4

Place the figs and stone fruits in a bowl, sprinkle with the cinnamon, add the orange juice, and toss well.

Heat a griddle pan until it is very hot. Cook the fruits for 1 to 2 minutes on each side until charred and slightly softened. Remove and set aside to cool.

Spoon the yogurt into bowls, top with the griddled fruits, grapes, and nuts, and finish with a thick slick of honey.

Delicious things on toast

Grape molasses & tahini

A killer flavor combination that I find completely addictive. Grape molasses is made from grape juice that has been concentrated, boiled down to make a thick, dark, and glossy syrup. It's a popular traditional sweetener in the Eastern Mediterranean and the Middle East, where it is often eaten at breakfast with some nuts and bread. You'll find it served as part of a traditional Turkish breakfast, commonly paired with tahini. You can either spread the tahini on toast and top with grape molasses, or tear off a chunk of bread and dip it in a bowl of tahini and the molasses. You can also substitute the grape molasses with date syrup, which has a similar flavor. Either way, it is delicious.

Kaymak, honey, & walnuts

Kaymak is a thick, luscious Turkish cream made from buffalo milk, which has some affinity with clotted cream. It is hugely popular in Turkey, where there are whole shops dedicated to different kinds of it, and it's my favorite part of a traditional Turkish breakfast, served with a slab of honeycomb or other good-quality honey and some fresh walnuts. Simply assemble all three on some good bread and you'll be in heaven.

Jams

While you'll find plenty of fruit conserves in Turkey, Cyprus, and Greece, the jams there tend to focus on larger pieces of fruit preserved in syrup. You can serve these in the mornings with bread and butter, or with a cup of black tea and a small spoon as a "spoon sweet," a sweet bite after a meal. The recipes on the next page will fill one medium or two small jars and I recommend keeping them in the refrigerator. Make sure you sterilize your jars before you pot jam in them. I do this by washing them with hot water and soap, then placing them in a low oven at around 275°F/140°C for about 10 minutes.

Sour cherry jam

1 lb 2 oz/500g frozen or fresh sour cherries (pitted
    weight)
2¾ cups/350g granulated sugar
7 tablespoons/100ml water
1 tablespoon lime juice

If you are using frozen cherries, they will
already be pitted, but if you are using fresh
cherries, you'll need to pit them. To do this,
wear an apron or an item of clothing you
don't mind getting cherry juice on and take
an empty wine bottle (or similar-shaped bottle)
and a chopstick. Place a cherry on the rim
of the bottle, hold it in place with your fingers
and use your other hand to firmly push the
chopstick through it to remove the pit.
It should pop straight through into the bottle.
Repeat with all your cherries.

Place the cherries, sugar, water, and lime juice
in a saucepan over low heat, stirring regularly
until the cherries have released enough liquid
to prevent the sugar from caramelizing.

Increase the heat to medium and bring the jam
to a rolling boil for about 30 minutes. It may
seem like there is a lot of liquid in the pan, but
don't worry as it will thicken considerably when
it cools.

Transfer to hot sterilized jars and seal tightly.
Once cooled, store in the refrigerator, where it
will keep for a few months.

Apricot jam

1 lb 2 oz/500g fresh apricots, pitted
2¾ cups/350g granulated sugar
¼ cup/60ml water
2 teaspoons lemon juice

Place a small plate in the freezer; you will
use this to test your jam once it has cooked.

Cut the apricots in rough 1¼-inch/3cm chunks;
you don't need to be too precise. If they are
small, it might be just a case of cutting them in
half and quartering them.

Place the apricots, sugar, and water in a
saucepan over medium heat. When the sugar
has dissolved, bring to a rolling boil and cook
for 15 minutes. As the mixture thickens and
reduces, stir frequently to make sure the jam
isn't burning on the bottom of the pan.

When the jam looks thick and slightly jelled,
turn off the heat and put a dollop of it on the
chilled plate. Return it to the freezer for a few
minutes, then do the "nudge test" with a finger:
if the jam mounds and wrinkles, it's done.
If not, continue to cook, then re-test the
jam until it reaches that consistency.

Once done, stir in the lemon juice and ladle
the hot jam into hot, sterilized jars. Seal tightly
and let cool to room temperature before
storing in the refrigerator, where it will keep
for a few months.

Sweet tahini swirls
TAHİNLİ ÇÖREK/TAHINOPITA

Tahini rolls are eaten throughout Greece, Turkey, and Cyprus, often grabbed from a street vendor early in the morning and washed down with a cup of strong black coffee. This version leans toward the Cypriot type, with its crisper feel from the tahini oozing out of the pastry. Because jars of tahini can separate into oil and solids if they've been open for a while, I recommend blending any separated mixture together again, or you risk the tahini filling being too runny or too hard. I use a spoon to crack through the solid tahini, then whiz it in a mini food processor with some of its separated oil. These rolls can be stored for up to three days in an airtight container, but, if you aren't eating them immediately, it's best to reheat them briefly. They also freeze well; you can pop them straight into the oven from frozen and heat at low temperature for ten minutes.

For the rolls
2⅓ cups/300g white bread flour, plus more to dust
1½ tablespoons fast-acting dried yeast
½ teaspoon salt
1 teaspoon granulated sugar
½ cup plus 2 tablespoons/150ml lukewarm whole milk
2 tablespoons lukewarm water
1 large egg, at room temperature, lightly beaten
5 tablespoons/75ml sunflower oil, or any other flavorless oil

For the filling
7 tablespoons/125g tahini
½ cup plus 2 tablespoons/125g granulated sugar
¾ teaspoon ground cinnamon

For the glaze
1 egg yolk, lightly beaten
1 teaspoon granulated sugar
white sesame seeds

MAKES 8

Place the flour, yeast, salt, and sugar in a bowl and stir to mix. Make a well in the middle and pour in the lukewarm milk and water, the egg, and oil. Knead the dough on a lightly floured work surface for 10 to 12 minutes until it is smooth and elastic. Place in a bowl, cover with plastic wrap or a damp tea towel, and let rise in a warm place for 1 to 1½ hours until doubled in size.

Spoon the tahini, sugar, and cinnamon for the filling into a bowl and mix to a thick paste. (If the tahini has separated, blitz it together first; see recipe introduction.) Line a baking sheet with parchment paper.

On a lightly floured surface, divide the dough into 8 pieces. Take a piece of dough, roll it into a ball, then squash it into a round disc about the size of your palm. Spoon 1 teaspoon of the tahini mixture onto the disc of dough and spread it out until it covers the center of it. Now pinch the sides of the dough inward, so the tahini paste is incorporated, and squash the dough flat into a disc again. Repeat on the other side. The aim of this process is to incorporate layers of tahini into the dough.

Now use your hands to stretch and mold the dough into a long sausage shape through gradual rolling and pulling to elongate it until you have a thin roll around 10 inches/25cm long and 1¼ inches/3cm wide. Don't worry if it starts to break or the tahini leaks out a bit as it all adds to the texture of the final pastry.

Once you have stretched it out as far as you can, use a knife to spread a little more tahini mixture all along the top of the roll of pastry, then gently twirl the 2 ends until it forms a loose spiral

Continued on the next page

a bit like a cheese straw. Finally, roll this spiral into a coil and use your palm to press it down and flatten it out.

Place the tahini roll on the prepared baking sheet and repeat with the remaining pieces of dough, leaving about 1 inch/a few centimeters between each one (you can arrange them on 2 sheets, if you need more room). Once you have prepared them all, let rest for 20 minutes and preheat the oven to 350°F/180°C.

Mix the egg yolk and sugar together, then brush the top and sides of the pastries with the mixture. Sprinkle sesame seeds on top of each bun, then bake on the middle shelf of the oven for 20 to 25 minutes, or until cooked through and golden brown.

Let cool for 20 minutes before serving.

Cardamom egg toast

Who doesn't like sweet and fluffy eggy bread, topped with cream or sweet syrup? This is my Eastern Mediterranean twist on a brunch classic. You should probably plan some time to digest on the sofa afterward.

4 large eggs
½ cup/120ml whole milk
4 teaspoons granulated sugar
large pinch of salt
seeds from 3 green cardamom
    pods, ground (¼ teaspoon)
4 thick slices of white bread
    or brioche
3 tablespoons/40g butter
2 tablespoons sunflower oil
confectioners' sugar, to dust

For the toppings (all optional)
date molasses or grape molasses
    and tahini
strawberries and kaymak

SERVES 2

Crack the eggs into a large shallow bowl, add the milk, sugar, salt, and crushed cardamom and lightly whisk with a fork.

Soak the slices of bread in the egg mixture for a couple of minutes on each side.

Melt half the butter and oil in a large frying pan over medium heat and, when it is hot, add 2 slices of the bread. Cook for a few minutes without moving until it is golden, then flip over and cook the other side. Remove from the pan and use a small sieve to dust with confectioners' sugar to taste.

Serve immediately with date or grape molasses and tahini, or fruit and *kaymak*, while you cook the remaining toasts in the remaining butter and oil.

Fragrant oats with rose water

My go-to breakfast whenever I'm in need of soothing, as the delicate blend of rose and cardamom offers heart-warming comfort. I only ever buy Iranian rose water—which I think is unmatched for its subtlety and lightness of flavor—but Lebanese brands are also good. What really brings the dish together, though, is the date syrup, which has a rich, treacle-like depth, so don't leave it out. Lots of people say oats don't fill them up for long, but that's because they aren't adding enough fat. Without a decent amount of fat and protein, your GI will spike after eating porridge and you'll get a sugar crash after a few hours. So stir in tablespoons of butter, coconut oil, or olive oil and bump up the protein with seeds and nuts. That way, it's guaranteed to keep you going until lunchtime.

1 cup/80g rolled oats
1¼ cups/300ml milk of your choice
1¼ cups/300ml water
seeds from 2 green cardamom
    pods, ground
¼ teaspoon ground cinnamon
¼ teaspoon salt
4 large dates, pitted and chopped
1 teaspoon rose water
2 tablespoons fat, such as olive
    oil, coconut oil, or butter
    (optional, but recommended,
    see recipe introduction)
2 tablespoons/30g ground
    flaxseeds, or other seeds or nuts
date syrup, to serve

SERVES 2

Place the oats, milk, and water in a saucepan over medium heat. Add the cardamom, cinnamon, and salt, then simmer for about 5 minutes until the oats soften. The more you stir, the creamier your porridge will be.

Add the dates and rose water and cook for another minute or so until the dates are warmed through. (If you want to add some extra fat, then this is the time to do it!)

Spoon into serving bowls, top with ground flaxseeds, and finish with a drizzle of date syrup.

Eggs with yogurt & chile butter

ÇILBIR

My favorite Turkish brunch dish: creamy, garlic-infused yogurt topped with poached eggs and chile butter. As the strength of garlic can be a matter of personal taste—especially in the morning—go easy with the amount you use the first time you make this. The garlic flavor shouldn't be overpowering, so add it in stages and taste as you go. For poached eggs to come out well the eggs need to be as fresh as possible, so for me this means keeping them in the refrigerator is a must . . . but I know the jury is out on that. Serve with buttered toast.

⅔ cup/200g strained Greek-style
   yogurt
¼–½ garlic clove, crushed
2 tablespoons salted butter
¼ teaspoon *pul biber* (Aleppo
   pepper), plus more to serve
½ teaspoon white wine vinegar,
   or apple cider vinegar
2 extra-large eggs
pinch of sumac
salt and black pepper
buttered toast, to serve (optional)

SERVES 2
as part of a Turkish breakfast,
or 1 hungry person on its own

Spoon the yogurt into a small shallow serving bowl and stir in the garlic and ¼ teaspoon salt.

Place some paper towel over a large plate so you can drain the eggs after they are cooked.

Melt the butter in a saucepan until it starts to sizzle. Add the *pul biber*, then take the pan off the heat.

Half-fill a small saucepan with just-boiled water and place it over medium heat. Add ¼ teaspoon salt and the vinegar. Crack the eggs into 2 separate cups or ramekins. Use a spoon to stir the water in the saucepan until you have a whirling pool. Quickly and gently drop the eggs into this spinning water, one by one. Then lower the heat and let the eggs cook for a few minutes until the whites are set. You can usually tell when the eggs are done because they rise to the top of the pan.

If you are eating this with bread, now is the time to stick it in the toaster and butter it.

When your eggs are ready, use a slotted spoon to transfer them to the paper towel–covered plate. Once the water has drained off, gently place them on top of the garlicky yogurt in the bowl, pour the chile butter over the top, sprinkle generously with salt and pepper, and finish with a smattering of sumac. Serve with toast.

Spiced tomato scramble

MENEMEN

This is one of the most iconic Turkish egg dishes and its name appears to have been derived from the Greek word *menemenos*, meaning to "flood" or "overflow." This makes sense when you see a pan of menemen with its eggs flooded in juicy, sweet tomatoes, just waiting for you to scoop up with some freshly baked *Pide ekmek* (see page 72).

Just to clarify, before you find yourself saying it, this is *not* a Turkish version of shakshuka. All countries in the Eastern Mediterranean and Middle East have their own versions of eggs cooked in tomatoes, and it does a disservice to the many food cultures of the region to lump them all together. Anyway, you don't need to get into regional politics over breakfast; just serve this with toasted bread, feta, and maybe a few slices of fried *sujuk* sausage (see page 60) and everyone will be happy. You can make the tomato sauce ahead of time too; it keeps well in the refrigerator for a few days.

2 tablespoons vegetable oil
1 tablespoon salted butter
½ small onion, finely chopped (around 3½ oz/100g)
6 large ripe tomatoes (total weight about 1 lb 5 oz/600g)
1 fat garlic clove, minced
½ red bell pepper, finely chopped
½ teaspoon dried oregano
½ teaspoon paprika
½ teaspoon *pul biber* (Aleppo pepper), plus more (optional) to serve
½ teaspoon granulated sugar
5 large eggs
leaves from a few herb sprigs, chopped, such as parsley, cilantro, or chives (optional)
salt and black pepper

SERVES 2

Melt the oil and butter in a sauté pan or deep frying pan over medium heat. Add the onion and fry for about 10 minutes, stirring occasionally.

Meanwhile, skin the tomatoes. To do this, use a knife to cut a cross into the top of them (where the stem was), then pop them into a bowl of just-boiled water. After 2 minutes, fish them out and you should be able to peel the skins off easily. If not, pop them back in the water for another minute. Once you've skinned the tomatoes, very finely chop them.

Once the onion is soft and golden, add the garlic and red pepper and fry for another couple of minutes. Add the tomatoes, oregano, paprika, *pul biber*, sugar, ½ teaspoon salt, and ¼ teaspoon black pepper and cook for another 5 minutes, uncovered. Lower the heat, cover, and simmer for 10 minutes, stirring occasionally so it cooks evenly.

Crack the eggs into a bowl and lightly whisk with a fork. Then add these to the pan of tomatoes and increase the heat a little. Let the eggs cook for 1 minute, then mix them in with a wooden spoon for 3 to 4 minutes until just set.

When the eggs are ready, serve them immediately with toast, a little sprinkle more *pul biber* if you like your eggs with some kick, and some chopped herbs, if you have any around.

Sujuk & eggs
SUCUKLU YUMURTA

Sujuk is a spicy cured beef sausage that is very popular in Turkey, either grilled and served as an appetizer or mezze, or fried with some sunny-side-up eggs. You can find it in most Mediterranean or Middle Eastern stores, but if you can't track any down, you can substitute another cured spicy sausage such as merguez or chorizo. To save on washing up, cook this in a small frying pan that can double up as a serving dish.

2 tablespoons vegetable oil
3 oz/80g *sujuk* sausage, sliced into
   thin discs
2 eggs
salt and black pepper
pinch of *pul biber* (Aleppo
   pepper), to serve

SERVES 2
as part of a Turkish breakfast,
or 1 hungry person on its own

Heat the oil in a small frying pan over medium heat. Add the sliced *sujuk* and cook for 1 to 2 minutes on each side, until it begins to crisp up.

Carefully crack the eggs over the sausages, season with a little salt and black pepper, then decrease the heat to low. Cover the pan with a lid (or use a plate if necessary) and cook until the yolks are just set, which should take a couple of minutes. To encourage the yolks to lightly cook, I tip the pan and spoon some of the oil over them a few times during this process.

Remove the pan from the heat and scatter with *pul biber* just before serving.

HONEYBEES
ATHENS, GREECE

As my time in Athens continues, I realize I need to ease myself into a better relationship with the city, and for that companionship always helps. So I feel very lucky to connect with Carolina Doriti, a warm chef, food writer, and bureau chief for Culinary Backstreets in Athens, a storytelling platform that reports from what they call "the borderless urban zone," sharing stories of a city's foodways as a way of better understanding a place and the people who live there. We instantly bond as she walks me around the city's food markets and specialty food stores, chatting about Greece's cuisine, food culture, and its recent social and political history.

Together we eat marinated anchovies and mussels at the central fish market, buy bunches of dried wild herbs at family-run delis and feast on beef *kavurma* and braised octopus at Ama Laxei, one of my favorite restaurants in the city. With Carolina's tips scribbled on notes in my back pocket, later I set off exploring on my own, wandering ancient ruins, sharing with friends plates of roasted goat drizzled with honey, and zucchini flower dolma, eating late-night falafels, and drinking fresh pomegranate juice.

But, of course, I am here to learn about more than just the food. As the week goes on, I pass demonstrations in squares calling for justice for migrants and I hear how this city and this country are recovering from the double hit of an economic crisis and a refugee crisis and yet, still, seem to manage to be more generous, open, and demonstrative of social solidarity than many of their European counterparts. There is no clearer example of this than Melissa, a women's refugee organization and community center, based just a short walk from where I am staying.

Melissa is a drop-in center for migrant and refugee women, offering a safe space in which to meet and socialize, as well as providing free courses and programs to help them develop their skills and talents. The word *melissa* means "honeybee" in Greek and the center operates as a beehive for women from all over the world. In beehives, the worker bees are always female and the name Melissa was chosen as a metaphor for female empowerment.

As I walk into the building, a sense of familiarity washes over me. There is something inherently comforting about women-only spaces and the feeling of safety that arises in them. Groups of women chat in Arabic and Dari on the sofa, hand-crafted artwork hangs on the walls, bookcases are filled with feminist texts in a variety of languages, and bunches of flowers are dotted around the tables. I am greeted with warm, expansive smiles from the staff. "Oh hi!" "Come in, welcome, *salaam*, do you want some tea?" "You can hang out over there, we're about to have lunch, take a seat."

I drop my bags and walk down a flight of stairs to the kitchen where I find two women standing over a stovetop, the smell of cilantro and cumin filling the air. One of the women introduces herself as Maria Ohilebo, a co-founder of Melissa who is in charge of its kitchen, where a free lunch is cooked daily for the women who visit. Today's menu is a chickpea stew and some jollof rice. "What do you think of this?" she asks, thrusting a spoon in my direction. "Enough salt?" Steam rushes off the chickpeas hovering in front of me and I take a bite. "Yes! It's delicious!" I exclaim and Maria nods firmly, turning back to her cooking pot, smiling. She already knew it was seasoned enough, she just wanted to make me feel included.

I take my plate of rice and stew back to the lounge where I spend the next hour sitting on the sofas and talking to women from Iran, Afghanistan, the Philippines, Syria, all sharing different experiences but with the same basic story: a desire for a better life, a difficult journey, the relief of finding Melissa, a spark of joy returning to their lives as they connect with other women in this sanctuary. Over cups of tea and pieces of sesame and honey brittle we discuss their hopes for their future lives and they tell me of their plans to become bakers, entrepreneurs, teachers, restaurateurs, politicians. The air fills with the excitement of possibility.

Soon Nadina Christopoulou, another co-founder of the project, calls me into her office, pouring us cups of coffee as we settle into our seats. "We wanted to create a space that brought women together to deal with their trauma," she tells me. "To get support, and then start thinking about what kind of future could be possible for them." I tell her it is evident to see that it is working, recalling a conversation I'd had with an Iranian woman over lunch who was setting up a food business in Athens.

"Yes," Nadina continues. "Despite the adversities these women have faced and continue to face, migrant women are incredibly resourceful. They are capable of making something out of almost nothing and multiplying their scarce resources in order to feed, nurture, and care for their families. A lot

of the work we do is based on building trust and community to make them feel safe enough to start that journey. And that, for us, is intrinsically linked with food."

"In what ways?" I ask.

"Oh, in many ways," Nadina says. "Food is the simplest way for people to communicate. One thing you notice if you spend time here is that there's an immense fluctuation of emotion throughout the day. In one morning, you laugh, you cry, you hug, you feel hopeful, you feel mad, you get angry . . . it's unrelenting. But with all those diverse emotions, the one thing that can help calm you down and soothe you is to sit with people, share food, and share your stories. To find the points of connection and empathy. For us, food is the one thing that we always make sure there is plenty of, because it creates a sense of comfort and home. It's a way for people who have obstacles in terms of language to communicate who they are, and to share their identity. The smell and the texture of the food open up not only your memory channels, but also your heart."

I ask Nadina to share an example of a campaign they have run with food and she tells me about Breakfast at the Park.

"This was at the time when the first refugees started arriving," she says. "Many were sleeping out in the parks. So we started an initiative to take a container and fill it with different things we had in our cupboards. It had to be something we had made, not store bought. Like a chicken salad sandwich or a slice of cake, or some olives and cheese and bread. It's easy to go and buy food, but we wanted to convey the message that somebody cares for you. Cares enough to spend their afternoon baking cake that smells like or feels like home."

Walking back from Melissa that evening, I realize that I need to take refuge for a while, to deal with my own grief and loss, before embarking on a new journey. By the time I arrive back at my apartment in Athens, I know I need to leave the city. I pack my bags and book a ferry ticket for the next day. It is time to head to the islands.

BREADS & GRAINS

Living in the vibrant and diverse neighborhood of Hackney, Northeast London, has many benefits, but being able to access incredible Turkish breads at any time of the day or night is definitely a major perk. Across the street from my home is a twenty-four-hour newsagent-slash-grocery shop where I often stop off in the mornings to pick up a large oval-shaped loaf of Turkish yeasted flatbread, eaten as an accompaniment to many of my favorite meals, from breakfast eggs to lentil soups to braised bean stews. Sometimes I am tempted by the rings of sesame-encrusted *simit* bread, sweet and crunchy with the chewiness of a bagel, which are perfect alongside cubes of feta and sliced tomatoes for lunch. Other times I grab half a dozen whole wheat pockets of pita, ready to be toasted and run through a tub of pink taramasalata. Or, if I'm feeling fancy, one of the shop's enriched doughs filled with pieces of olives, or flaky pastries stuffed with spinach. The choice is as endless as it is bewitching.

. . . .

For a hungry eater, one of the joys of Eastern Mediterranean food is that it doesn't shy away from bringing double carbs to the table, and bread is always served to accompany a meal, as essential an accompaniment as salt and pepper. Rice is also commonplace, served plain or in pilafs and always seasoned with plenty of butter, giving a richness and depth of flavor that means you can happily eat it on its own, with perhaps just a spoonful of yogurt on the side.

Bread is revered in Turkish culture; folklore has it that, if a piece of bread accidently falls on the ground, it must be picked up immediately and placed somewhere higher (some people even kiss the loaf as a mark of respect). Stale bread is never thrown away, but rather upcycled and added as a thickener to dips, or used to add substance to meatballs, giving it a second lease on life. Whole books could be written about the breads and grains of the region, so what follows is a modest selection of some of my favorites from my travels, all of which are perfect for soaking up the flavorsome oils and juices of Eastern Mediterranean food.

Turkish flatbread

PİDE EKMEK

A classic Turkish flatbread to accompany all meals, from fried eggs to lentil soup to taramasalata dip. These are best eaten on the day you bake them, however you can also freeze them and simply reheat in a toaster or a low oven. You'll need a couple of large baking sheets or pizza stones to cook them, as they are quite big.

1½ cups plus 1 tablespoon/375ml lukewarm water
1 envelope (2¼ teaspoons/7g) fast-acting dried yeast
2 teaspoons granulated sugar
4 cups/500g white bread flour, plus more to dust
1½ teaspoons salt
3 tablespoons olive oil, plus more for oiling
1 egg yolk
½ teaspoon nigella seeds

MAKES 2 MEDIUM LOAVES / SERVES 6 as part of a mezze

Take 3 tablespoons of the lukewarm water and place in a cup with the yeast and sugar. Stir well and set aside for 5 minutes.

Place the flour and salt in a large bowl. Make a well in the center, then pour in the yeast mixture, the remaining lukewarm water, and the oil.

Use your hands to mix the dough together. It will be very wet to begin with but, as you continue, the consistency will change. Knead for 5 minutes, then let it rest for 10 minutes. Finally, knead it again for 10 to 15 minutes until smooth and elastic. To tell your dough is ready, give it a firm poke. If the indentation you make fills quickly, it's done. If the dent stays, continue kneading. Or do the "windowpane test": take a small piece of dough and stretch it so you get a thin, almost translucent square (like a windowpane). If you can stretch the dough thin without it breaking, it's ready. If not, knead for a few more minutes.

Brush a large bowl with oil, place in the ball of dough, and turn to lightly coat. Cover with plastic wrap or a damp tea towel and set in a warm place for 1 to 1½ hours, or until doubled in size.

Turn it onto a lightly floured surface and cut it in half. Tear off 2 large sheets of parchment paper then, with floured hands, stretch each piece of dough into a large oval on each sheet. Aim for each to measure about 13 x 6½ inches/33 x 17cm and ½ to ¾ inch/1 to 2 cm thick. Cover with damp tea towels and set aside for 30 minutes in a warm place to rise for the second time.

Preheat the oven to 425°F/220°C and place 2 baking sheets or pizza stones inside to warm up.

Whisk the egg yolk with 1 tablespoon olive oil. Brush the loaves with this, then make indentations with your fingers so they look as if they have dimples. Sprinkle with the nigella seeds, then slide onto the hot sheets or pizza stones and bake for 15 to 18 minutes, until golden and hollow-sounding when you tap the bottoms.

Olive bread

ELIOPITA

Cypriot olive bread is enriched with olive oil, giving it a lovely soft crumb that melds perfectly with the salty black olives and sweet onions. It's a very flavorsome bread on its own, so can be served as an appetizer with a small bowl of good-quality extra-virgin olive oil to dunk pieces in, or as an accompaniment to simpler mezze dishes.

½ small onion (about 3½ oz/100g), finely chopped
½ cup/100g Kalamata olives, pitted and roughly chopped
4 cups/500g white bread flour
1½ teaspoons salt
6 tablespoons/90ml light olive oil, plus 2 tablespoons more to fry
1 envelope (2¼ teaspoons/7g) fast-acting dried yeast
1 cup plus 2 tablespoons/275ml lukewarm water

MAKES 2 LOAVES /
SERVES 4 TO 6
as part of a mezze

Fry the onion in 2 tablespoons olive oil for about 15 minutes over low heat, until soft and translucent. Transfer to a bowl, add the chopped olives, and let cool.

Place the flour, salt, olive oil, and yeast in a large bowl (taking care not to put the yeast in direct contact with the salt when they are first added to the bowl). Add the water, one-third at a time, mixing until you have a sticky dough. Knead the dough with your hands and knuckles until it is elastic, smooth, and shiny. This should take 10 to 12 minutes. Test to see if the dough is ready (see page 72).

Divide the dough in half and work half of the onion-olive mixture into each piece, using your hands to gently fold it into the bread. It may seem like a struggle to get them in initially, but keep poking the olives and onions into gaps in the dough and you'll get there after a few minutes. Don't worry if it tears a bit, or if pieces fall out, it will even out after rising.

When the onions and olives have all been incorporated, place the 2 dough balls in separate bowls, cover with plastic wrap or a tea towel, and let rise in a warm place until they have doubled in size. Depending on the heat and humidity in your kitchen, this can take 1 to 1½ hours.

When the dough has risen, line a baking sheet with parchment paper, then stretch each piece of dough out to form a narrow loaf around 12 x 4 inches/30 x 10cm.

Preheat the oven to 400°F/200°C and bake the bread for 30 to 40 minutes until golden brown.

Spiced cornbread with feta

MISIR EKMEĞİ

This recipe is inspired by a lunch I ate with Hatice Anne, a cook in Istanbul who grew up in the Black Sea region of Turkey. Hatice runs a small café on the Asian side of the Bosporus, which specializes in Black Sea recipes such as cornbread. Her version was made with just oil, yogurt, egg, and salt, but I couldn't help adding salty white cheese and Turkish spices. You can find fine cornmeal in South Asian and Turkish grocery stores, or in the "world food" sections of larger supermarkets. This is best served on the day you bake it. I often cook it in a cast-iron ovenproof frying pan (around 9 inches/23cm wide) so it can go straight from the oven to the table, but a small baking pan will work just as well.

5 tablespoons/75 ml olive oil,
   plus more for the pan
1½ cups/220g fine cornmeal
1¼ cups/160g all-purpose flour
1 teaspoon baking powder
½ teaspoon baking soda
1½ teaspoons cumin seeds,
   toasted and ground
½ teaspoon sweet paprika
1 tablespoon granulated sugar
1 cup/240ml whole milk
¾ cup/180g plain yogurt
2 extra-large eggs, lightly beaten
1 tablespoon lemon juice
3 green onions, finely chopped
¾ cup/125g feta cheese, roughly
   crumbled
large handful of parsley,
   finely chopped
salt and white pepper

SERVES 4 TO 6

Preheat the oven to 400°F/200°C. Generously oil a 9-inch/23cm cast-iron skillet or round baking pan.

Mix the cornmeal, flour, baking powder, baking soda, cumin, paprika, sugar, 1½ teaspoons salt, and ¼ teaspoon white pepper in a large bowl.

Whisk the milk, yogurt, eggs, olive oil, and lemon juice in another bowl.

Stir the wet ingredients into the dry ingredients and mix well to make sure everything is fully combined. Finally, fold in the green onions, feta, and herbs.

Pour the batter into the prepared pan. Bake for 30 to 35 minutes, or until golden brown.

Let cool for 15 minutes before serving.

Pita bread

A classic of the region, these soft pockets of bread are perfect for stuffing with *köfte* or kebabs, or running through a bowl of fava (see page 110). They are best eaten soon after you have made them, but also freeze well. So if you aren't eating them on the day you've baked them, I recommend popping them in the freezer. I make no apology for having published this recipe before, as it's a keeper.

2 cups/250g white bread
    flour, plus more to dust
2 teaspoons fast-acting
    dried yeast
¼ teaspoon granulated sugar
1 teaspoon salt
⅔ cup/160ml lukewarm water
1 tablespoon extra-virgin olive
    oil, plus more for oiling

MAKES 6

If you are using a stand mixer fitted with a dough hook, place the flour, yeast, sugar, and salt in its mixing bowl. Add half the water and all the olive oil. Knead for 5 minutes on medium speed, or until the dough comes together in a ball. Every minute after this, gradually add a little of the remaining water, until all the flour has come away from the sides and you have a soft dough. (You may not need all the water.)

If kneading by hand, follow the process above but, once you've mixed all the ingredients together in a bowl, place the dough on a lightly floured surface and knead for about 10 minutes. The dough will be wet in the beginning, but keep going and it will become smooth, stretchy, and pliable.

Test to see if the dough is ready (see page 72). If not, keep kneading it for a few more minutes.

When the dough is ready, use your fingertips to smooth its surface with a drop of olive oil, lightly coating it. Place in a large bowl, cover with plastic wrap, and let rise in a warm place for about 1 hour, or until doubled in size.

Knock the air out of the dough by firmly whacking it on the work surface a few times. Cut it into 6 equal-size balls. Using a rolling pin, roll each piece of dough into an oval about ¼ inch/5mm thick. Cover with a clean, damp tea towel and let rise for a final 15 minutes.

Meanwhile, preheat the oven to its highest setting. Lightly dust a pizza stone or 2 baking sheets with a little flour (this prevents the bread from sticking) and place in the oven to heat up. Place the flatbreads on the hot stone or sheets; you will probably have to cook them in batches. Cook for 3 to 5 minutes, until just puffed up and starting to color. Cover with a clean cloth until cool, while you cook the remaining breads. Serve as soon as possible, or at least within a few hours.

Orzo rice

ŞEHRİYELİ PİLAV

This buttery rice flecked with toasted orzo pasta is a Turkish staple and my favorite accompaniment to many of the dishes in this book. Traditionally it is made with baldo rice, a Turkish short-grain variety you can find online or in Turkish grocery stores. You can substitute white calrose rice or white basmati rice if necessary.

1¾ cups/360g baldo white rice
   (or calrose, or basmati)
1 tablespoon salted butter
1 tablespoon vegetable oil
3 tablespoons orzo pasta
3¼ cups/770ml just-boiled water
salt

SERVES 4 TO 6

Rinse the rice in cold water until the water runs clear, then place it in a large bowl of cold water and let soak for 15 minutes. Drain and set aside.

Melt the butter and oil in a medium saucepan over medium heat until it starts to sizzle. Add the orzo and cook for 2 to 3 minutes until the pasta starts to turn golden brown. Then add the drained rice and stir until it is well coated in the butter and the orzo is evenly distributed. Sauté for 3 minutes.

Pour in the hot water and ¾ teaspoon salt. Lay 3 to 4 pieces of paper towel or a clean tea towel over the pan, then place the lid tightly on top, decrease the heat to low, and cook for 12 minutes. Don't lift the lid off during the cooking time, as you want it to steam.

After 12 minutes, check to see the rice is cooked by running a spoon through to check all the grains and tasting some of it. If it needs a few more minutes, replace the lid and cook for a little longer. If not, take off the heat and let rest for 10 minutes with the lid on, before running a fork through it to fluff it up before serving.

Tomato & mint dolma

YAPRAK SARMA

In my many years of eating stuffed grape leaves, this Cypriot version made with plum tomatoes and spearmint may be my favorite. Don't be put off by the physical task of stuffing and rolling, as these are relatively straightforward to make and the process has a meditative quality too, so I recommend making a batch during times of stress. (I made them repeatedly in the first weeks of the COVID-19 lockdown, but that's another story.) I didn't grow up learning how to make stuffed grape leaves, so used to find them a bit intimidating. Thankfully, during the course of writing this book, I think I've finally cracked it. The tricks are to not overfill the leaves, to roll them tightly, and to approach each one with utter confidence.

I was shown how to make these with yoga teacher Çizge Yalkın and her grandmother Nahide Köşkeroğlu; we stuffed half the mixture into zucchini flowers and, if you ever get the opportunity to use some, I highly recommend it. Otherwise, you can find brined grape leaves in just about any Middle Eastern or Mediterranean store. This recipe makes 30 to 35 dolma depending on the size of the leaves and I like to serve it with thick plain yogurt on the side. The dolma keep well in the refrigerator for about three days, in a covered container. I often warm them up in a saucepan with a drop of water, to take the chill off them if they've been refrigerated.

For the dolma
1 cup/200g Turkish baldo rice, or calrose (you can also use basmati)
1 small white onion, grated (about 7 oz/200g)
1¼ cups/270g canned whole peeled tomatoes, very finely chopped or blitzed in a food processor
1 tablespoon tomato paste
1 tablespoon dried mint
½ teaspoon ground cinnamon
2 tablespoons finely chopped mint leaves
3 tablespoons finely chopped parsley leaves
1 tablespoon lemon juice
5 tablespoons/75ml extra-virgin olive oil, plus more to drizzle
1 package or jar of brined grape leaves
salt and black pepper

Place all the ingredients for the filling in a large bowl with 1¼ teaspoons salt and ½ teaspoon black pepper and mix well.

Place 35 grape leaves in a large saucepan filled with just-boiled water. Simmer for 5 minutes over medium heat, then refresh under cold water.

Lay a grape leaf on a plate with the vein side up (snap off any stalks) and smooth it out. Then, depending on the size of the leaf, place 1½ to 3 teaspoons of the filling at the bottom and mold it into a rectangle, horizontal to you. Deftly and firmly roll the grape leaf over the stuffing, tucking the side flaps inward as you do so to ensure it is sealed at both ends and will prevent the parcel from opening while cooking. The juice will run out as you squeeze them but that doesn't matter, just collect it in a cup and add it to the cooking pan later.

Place the dolma in a large, shallow saucepan as you roll them and continue stuffing the leaves until all the filling has been used up. Don't worry if your dolma aren't a uniform shape or look a bit small, they will plump up after cooking and even out.

Continued on the next page

Tomato & mint dolma
continued

For the broth
1 tablespoon tomato paste
1 cup/240ml cold water
full-fat, strained plain yogurt,
  to serve

MAKES 30 TO 35
SERVES 6
as part of a mezze

Once all the stuffed leaves are in the pan, mix the tomato paste and water and pour it over the dolma. Drizzle with another 2 tablespoons olive oil, then place a dinner plate on top of the leaves to cover them and press them down.

Place the lid on the saucepan and set it over medium heat for a few minutes until the water comes to a boil (lift the plate to check underneath). Then decrease the heat to low and simmer for about 45 minutes.

Check a dolma to see if the rice is cooked. If the rice is still a little firm, or the water has all evaporated, add another 7 tablespoons/100ml or so of water, cover, and cook for another 10 minutes. If there is still broth in the pan, the dolma will soak it up as they cool.

Once ready, let cool in the pan for at least 15 minutes before serving. I personally prefer to give them longer, until they come to room temperature, and always accompany them with thick yogurt on the side.

Halloumi & mint muffins

Halloumi and mint are a classic Cypriot flavor combination and they meld so perfectly together. This recipe is inspired by my hosts at the Bougainvillea Guesthouse in North Nicosia, who greeted me with a plate of these when I checked in, tired and weary, after an international flight. They are fantastic picnic food, delicious eaten alongside a soup or a stew, or make a very tasty addition to a brunch table. I think they taste best on the day that you make them, but they will keep for a few days in an airtight container, or they also freeze well. As muffins need to be worked as little as possible so that their texture stays light, keep the amount of stirring you do to a minimum.

1⅓ cup/150g grated halloumi cheese
1⅓ cup plus 1 tablespoon/175g all-purpose flour
½ cup/50g whole wheat flour
2 teaspoons baking powder
1½ teaspoons nigella seeds
1½ teaspoons dried mint
2 large eggs, lightly beaten
7 tablespoons/100ml olive oil
⅔ cup/180g full-fat Greek-style yogurt
salt and white pepper

MAKES 12

Preheat the oven to 400°F/200°C and line a muffin pan with 12 paper liners.

Place the halloumi, both flours, the baking powder, nigella seeds, and mint in a large mixing bowl and add ¼ teaspoon each of salt and white pepper.

In a separate bowl, whisk together the eggs, oil, and yogurt, then stir them into the flour mixture until just combined. Do not overmix, or the muffins will be dense.

Spoon the batter into the muffin liners and bake for about 20 minutes, until the tops are golden and a toothpick inserted into the center of a muffin emerges clean.

Spinach, herb, & feta pie

SPANAKOPITA

I ate this more times that I can remember while traveling through Greece. It is perfect snack food when you are on the go and—with a few nice salads—makes a delicious light lunch or dinner too. I use several different kinds of leaves and herbs in this and you can adapt these to what is available to you, or just use spinach, as long as the overall amount of greens comes to around 3½ pounds/1.6kg. I make this in a rectangular roasting pan and cut it into large rectangles or squares for serving.

1 lb 2 oz/500g green chard
2 tablespoons sunflower oil
1 fat garlic clove, minced
3 green onions, finely sliced (about
    2½ oz/70g)
2 lb 2 oz/1kg fresh or frozen
    spinach, roughly chopped
2½ cups/50g parsley, roughly
    chopped
1¼ cups/25g dill, roughly chopped
1¼ cups/25g mint leaves, roughly
    chopped
finely grated zest of
    2 unwaxed lemons
2 extra-large eggs, lightly beaten
pinch of ground nutmeg
1⅓ cup/200g feta cheese, crumbled
about ¼ cup/60ml olive oil
12 filo pastry sheets
salt and black pepper

SERVES 4 TO 6
as part of a picnic or mezze

Separate the chard leaves from the stalks. Take half the stalks and chop them into small pieces (keep the remainder for soup).

Heat the sunflower oil in a large saucepan and add the chard stalks, garlic, green onions, and ½ teaspoon salt. Stir well, cover the pan, lower the heat, and cook for 5 minutes, stirring occasionally, until the stalks have softened. Add the chard leaves and cook for another 5 minutes with the lid on until they wilt, stirring occasionally.

Now add the spinach and herbs and cook for a couple of minutes until they wilt too. (If you can't fit them all in the same pan, you can cook them separately.) Transfer all the greens to a colander and let them cool for 10 minutes.

Preheat the oven to 400°F/200°C.

Using your hands, squeeze as much liquid as you can from the greens and transfer to a large mixing bowl. Stir in the lemon zest, eggs, nutmeg, ½ teaspoon salt, and a generous grind of black pepper. Finally, lightly fold in the feta.

Brush a 9 x 13-inch/23 x 33 cm roasting pan with olive oil. Lay out a sheet of filo on a work surface and brush it with oil too. Cover with another sheet of filo and repeat until you have 6 layers of filo brushed with oil and covering an area large enough to line the sides and bottom of your roasting pan, with extra overhanging the edges.

Line the dish with the oiled filo, fill it with the greens, and fold the excess pastry over the edges of the filling, trimming to create a ¾-inch/2cm border. Make another 6-layer filo piece as before and place on top. Scrunch up the pastry a little to create a wavy, uneven top and trim the edges so it just covers the filling.

Brush with more olive oil and bake for 40 minutes, until golden brown. Serve warm or at room temperature.

ISLANDS IN THE SEA
IKARIA, GREECE

The midday sun beats down on the port of Piraeus as I wait to board the ferry leaving Athens. Packed in my bag is a hefty square of spanakopita, a dense filo pastry filled with spinach, wild greens, and crumbled feta cheese. Beside it is a bag of purple grapes. Fortifying snacks to accompany me on the eight-hour boat journey to the Greek island of Ikaria.

Known as the "red rock" during the Greek Civil War of the 1940s, Ikaria is an island where more than 13,000 communists—among them prominent writers, artists, and musicians—were exiled by the Greek dictatorship. In the decades that followed, these exiles are said to have influenced the local islanders with their political and creative outlook. Ever since, the island has become a hub for alternative communities, attracting anarchists, artists, and hippies looking to forge a more communal way of life.

As well as its colorful political and social history, Ikaria is probably better known internationally for being one of the world's "Blue Zones," places where the local population live far longer than the global average. Ikaria has a disproportionally high number of centenarians and one in three people on the island live into their nineties. Diet and lifestyle are credited with these exceptional statistics and so, weary traveler that I am, Ikaria seems like a good place to reset and recharge en route to the islands of Samos and Lesvos.

The boat journey is slow and steady, surrounded by blues of all shades—the cornflower deck, the azure sea, the cobalt sky—and a gusty wind that hits us soon after we lose sight of shore. The inside of the boat feels uncomfortable, with hard plastic seats and annoyingly loud TVs, so I spend the journey on the deck. I roll out my sarong to make makeshift bedding over my luggage, eat my spinach pie, and pull my sunhat down over my eyes to take a nap.

I wake to the sound of music and clapping and a dramatically different view. Gone are the bright blues from earlier, the evening sky is now cut with orange, pink, and amber and the sea is a dark and murky shade of indigo.

I pull on a sweater and walk in the direction of the music coming from the far end of the boat. It doesn't take me long to find the man in the middle of a circle of people playing a *tsampouna*, a type of piped woodwind instrument that looks like it is made from lamb skin with a reed chanter. As he plays, a group of young Greeks dance the *kalamatianós*, one of Greece's most popular folk dances, holding hands as they move in an counterclockwise rotation, their feet tapping in time with the music. As I watch them, I am reminded of so many of the folk dances of this region and how this hand-held line dance, so rooted in Greek culture, is also found across Turkey, Cyprus, the Caucuses, the Middle East . . . It makes me think of my parents dancing at Iranian parties back in Birmingham, and I smile.

As the dancers circle, more and more people from around the ferry join the spectacle, clapping along with the music as they admire the silhouettes of the dancers against the backdrop of the burnt orange sunset. Not long after, it falls dark as the towering rocks of Ikaria pass alongside us. It feels as if we are being welcomed on to the island through a portal of music, dance, and song.

The weeks on the island pass quick and fast. I find an alternative community in an enclave in the North of the island and rent a small apartment with a kitchen so that I can cook the fresh produce I find at local markets. The laid-back pace of island life makes the slow, sleepy days blur into one. Mornings begin with thick Greek yogurt, seasonal fruits, and a slab of honeycomb collected by the owner of a nearby guest house. Lunch often involves a forty-minute walk to the neighboring village to buy long green beans, squash, dried fava, and fresh bread to make a simple lunch. Sometimes, too lazy to cook, I simply sit in a taverna eating baked parcels of feta drizzled with honey, grilled souvlaki, and a crisp Greek salad. Then a siesta and perhaps a swim before heading up to the rocks to watch the sunset.

Dusk falls as the cue for appetites to open and—with the hot sun gone—to eat the heavier dishes the island has to offer. Some nights it is pasta with a sauce of caramelized onions and pungent goat butter, or slow-roasted goat *kleftiko* with chunky potatoes, the island's specialty. Each Friday, a different village holds a fête with food and music, lining the streets with communal tables where we gather to eat roasted goat with an assortment of mezze washed down with local wine, against a background of a band playing folk music. If you are thinking that is a lot of goat for an Aegean island, you're not wrong. "Goat is our island's fish!" locals tell me proudly. It turns out that overfishing means there's very little fish or seafood left in the island's waters.

After a few weeks on the island, the secret to Ikarian longevity seems to be seasonal food, co-operative living, afternoon naps, hours of sunshine,

a day spent mostly outdoors, fresh fruit and vegetables, lots of walking, swimming, farming, and—just as important—socializing.

One morning I come into the front yard to see the elderly owner of the apartment I am renting carrying a huge crate of grapes to his courtyard. I watch as he pours the grapes into a plastic vat and then proceeds to step inside it, to stamp on them, pressing out the juices to make his very own wine. "The secret to a long life," he pauses, pointing at me, "is eating and drinking well!"

As he squelches the grapes between his toes, his wife guffaws, rolls her eyes, and pushes her hairband back across her gray hair. "Yes, that, and having someone to cook for you!"

MEZZE, LIGHT MEALS, & SIDES

There's an art to eating mezze in the Mediterranean and I'm still learning it. It goes something like this. You visit a restaurant with friends and all order a few dishes each. Then, over the course of a few hours, you leisurely eat, savoring each dish as it comes out, taking a couple of well-earned digestive rests in the middle, and always ordering more food than any of you can expect to eat in one sitting.

One night in Istanbul, I was taken for dinner at a popular *meyhane* (a word derived from the Persian for wine, *mey*, and house, *khaneh*). As the etymology suggests, this is a place where locals come to drink and eat, and where milky-white glasses of the anise-based spirit raki are sipped alongside hot and cold small plates such as stuffed mussels, braised artichokes, grilled sardines, and meat *köfte*. We ordered a selection of dishes and, as they started coming out, I piled them on my plate, greedily downing one delicacy after another, relishing the intimacy of picking the food up with my fingers and licking them clean after. After a while, I noticed my companion had hardly touched her plate and I started to feel embarrassed. I need not have worried; as the night wore on, she ate far more than I did, but, because she had paced herself, she was able to fit more in. It was a lesson that reminded me of the Turkish proverb, "If you are going a long way, go slowly." With food as good as this, you'd be a fool not to.

• •

This chapter features some of my favorite mezze, small plates and side dishes from the Eastern Mediterranean, with a strong emphasis on vegetables, pulses, and legumes. Many of the recipes have very subtle flavorings and so rely on the quality of the vegetables and olive oil to really shine. I know it isn't always possible (and it's not like I do it all the time), but if you can buy seasonal and organic produce when you can afford it, that will massively improve the flavor of the final dishes. Typically you'd want at least four dishes to make up a mezze, but you can mix and match, picking them from any of the chapters in the book.

Garlicky eggplant salad

YOĞURTLU PATLICAN SALATASI

Sitting somewhere between salad, side dish, and dip, this is one of those dishes that demonstrates that the best recipes are sometimes the simplest, and celebrates one of the region's favorite ingredients: the mighty eggplant. The flavors improve over time, so it's a good mezze to make ahead. I recommend scooping up the sweet eggplant with warm flatbreads, or serving it alongside grilled meats, roasted vegetables, or simmered beans.

3 large eggplants
(total weight about 2 lb 2 oz/1kg)
1 cup/245g full-fat Greek-style
yogurt
1 fat garlic clove, minced
1 tablespoon chopped parsley
leaves, plus more to serve
1 tablespoon extra-virgin
olive oil, plus more to serve
salt and black pepper

SERVES 4
as part of a mezze,
or as a side dish

Preheat the oven to 425°F/220°C.

Pierce each eggplant with a fork all over, then place on a baking sheet and roast for 1 hour, or until completely soft. You want the eggplants to completely collapse in on themselves and for the skins to be charred. Remove the eggplants from the oven, slice them in half with a knife and let cool.

Once they are completely cold, scoop out the eggplant flesh with a spoon.

Discard the eggplant skins and roughly chop any big pieces of eggplant pulp. Place this in a serving bowl and add the yogurt, garlic, parsley, ¾ teaspoon salt, ½ teaspoon black pepper, and the extra-virgin olive oil. Stir well with a fork to get everything evenly combined and then taste to adjust the seasoning (I often add a bit more salt at this stage, as I think the eggplants benefit from it).

Cover with a plate or plastic wrap and pop it in the refrigerator, letting it rest for at least 1 hour before serving. Finish with a drizzle of olive oil and a smattering of chopped parsley.

Spicy red pepper & walnut smash

MUHAMMARA

This spicy, smoky dip is most commonly associated with the Syrian city of Aleppo, but is popular throughout the Levant and Turkey. As levels of heat are a matter of personal taste, I recommend adjusting the *pul biber* to your preference. What's really important here is to use walnuts that are fresh, as they can turn rancid very quickly which makes them (and this dish) taste bitter. Serve with flatbreads, or as a condiment with grilled vegetables, fish, or meat.

3 red bell peppers (total weight about 1 lb/450g)
3 tablespoons extra-virgin olive oil, plus more to serve
1 cup/100g walnuts
1 garlic clove, crushed
3 tablespoons pomegranate molasses
1 to 2 tablespoons lemon juice
½ teaspoon sweet paprika, or smoked paprika, or to taste
¾ to 1 teaspoon *pul biber* (Aleppo pepper), or to taste
salt and black pepper
pomegranate seeds and / or finely chopped parsley leaves, to serve (optional)

SERVES 6
as part of a mezze

Preheat the oven to 400°F/200°C.

Halve the red bell peppers, scoop out the seeds, and slice off any white pith. Place on a baking sheet, drizzle with the olive oil and roast for around 30 minutes, until they are completely soft and their skins have blackened. Remove the peppers from the oven and allow them to cool slightly before peeling their skins off. (If you put them in a bowl covered with a plate to steam while they cool, the skins come off much more easily.)

To make the dip you can either use a food processor or a very large mortar and pestle, if you have one. I like this to have a chunkier texture, so opt for the latter. Either way, begin by pulsing/smashing the walnuts in a food processor or mortar and pestle until they resemble breadcrumbs. Then add three-quarters of the roasted peppers and pulse/smash these with the walnuts so they break up and form a rough dip (you want some texture here, so don't aim for a purée). Roughly chop the remaining roasted peppers and set aside.

Spoon the pulverized walnut and pepper mixture into a serving dish and add all the remaining ingredients, with ¾ teaspoon salt and ¼ teaspoon black pepper.

Stir well, then taste to adjust the seasoning, adding a touch more salt, paprika, or *pul biber* to taste.

Cover and let rest for 1 hour for the flavors to come together, then top with the reserved chopped roasted peppers and a little parsley or a handful of pomegranate seeds, if you like. Finish with a little flourish of extra-virgin olive oil.

For recipe photo, see page 98

Greek greens

HORTA

A stalwart of the Greek taverna, this rustic dish of braised wild greens is packed with flavor and, I swear, it makes you feel healthier just by looking at it. I've used greens that are most readily available to me, but I highly recommend adapting the recipe by using any seasonal, local wild greens of your choice. Dandelion, nettles, and beet tops all work well. The rest is down to the quality of your olive oil, so buy a good bottle and be generous with it. Serve at room temperature.

1 lb 2 oz/500g chard
9 oz/250g kale
2 cups/480ml just-boiled water
7 oz/200g spinach
5 cups/100g cilantro, leaves and
   stems
3 tablespoons lemon juice,
   or to taste
¼ cup/60ml extra-virgin
   olive oil
salt and black pepper

SERVES 4
as a side dish

Using a pair of kitchen scissors, remove the thick stalks from the chard and kale, then roughly chop their leaves. Place the leaves in a large saucepan, pour in the just-boiled water, and turn the heat on to high. Cover, then boil for 5 to 10 minutes until soft. (I like my greens very well cooked, but decrease the cooking time if you prefer.)

Add the spinach and cilantro and cook for a final 4 minutes.

Take the pan off the heat and drain the greens in a colander. Let cool for at least 10 minutes, giving them a bit of a stir every few minutes so the steam rises and they dry off.

Transfer the cooked greens to a serving bowl, then add the lemon juice, olive oil, ½ teaspoon salt, and ¼ teaspoon black pepper. Use your hands to toss the greens in the dressing until fully combined; you want to get all the leaves coated. Taste and adjust the seasoning and lemon juice to your preference.

For recipe photo, see page 242

Taramasalata

I make no apologies for the intensity of this dip; it's smoky, salty, fishy, and I love it. Traditionally made with the smoked roe of carp, grey mullet, or cod, it is eaten throughout Greece, Turkey, and Cyprus as an appetizer or a part of mezze spreads. If you want to lessen the intensity of the smoked fish, you can soak the roe in a bowl of cold water for a few hours, or add some yogurt or crème fraîche, which mellows the flavor. A batch of this will keep in the refrigerator for up to five days and I find that the flavors are much better after it's rested for a day or two, so I strongly suggest making it twenty-four hours in advance. Serve with olives and warm bread.

3½ oz/100g smoked cod's roe
3½ oz/100g stale or slightly toasted
    white bread, crusts removed
    (about 2 slices)
3 tablespoons lemon juice,
    or to taste
¼ cup/60ml sunflower oil
½ garlic clove, crushed
¼ cup/60ml water, or as needed
1 tablespoon plain yogurt
    (optional)
salt and black pepper

SERVES 4 TO 6
as part of a mezze

Peel the skin and any threads of membrane from the roe (you may want to use gloves for this). If you are wary of the strong smoked fish flavor, you can soak the roe in a large bowl of cold water for a couple of hours. Otherwise, place the roe straight into a food processor.

Fill a bowl with cold water and then immerse the slices of bread into it for a few seconds until they soften. Quickly lift the bread out, squeeze out any excess water and add to the food processor with the remaining ingredients. I often like to add the spoonful of yogurt to lighten the mixture and add a touch more creaminess.

Blend the dip until smooth, then taste it and adjust the seasoning. You may want a touch more lemon juice for acidity or water to loosen the mixture, or both.

Allow the flavors to come together for at least 3 hours or preferably overnight before serving.

Iranian eggplant & kashk dip

KASHK E BADEMJAN

This is one of Iran's most popular appetizers and finds itself in this book as an ode to Mozhdeh, an Afghan woman I met in Lesvos. Mozhdeh was one of many Afghans from Iran I met on the island and we spent an afternoon trawling through our favorite recipes before both firmly landing on this one. It's a bit of a labor of love, as it does take time and prep, but—as any Iranian will tell you—it's worth the effort. The unique flavor comes from *kashk*, a fermented yogurt that has some affinity to pungent goat cheese and that you can buy in Middle Eastern stores or online. *Kashk* comes in a variety of formats but, for this recipe, I recommend buying the jars of thick paste often mysteriously labeled as "Iranian sauce." This recipe keeps well in the refrigerator for three days, so you can make it ahead of time and simply warm it up and decorate just before serving. Serve warm with *lavaash* flatbread.

2 lb 14 oz/1.3kg (4 to 5 medium)
    eggplants
sunflower oil
2 small onions, finely chopped
    (around 12¼ oz/350g)
4 fat garlic cloves, crushed
½ teaspoon ground turmeric
1½ tablespoons dried mint
2 teaspoons lemon juice
1¼ cups/300ml just-boiled water
¼ cup/60ml *kashk* paste
salt and black pepper

For the toppings
2 tablespoons roughly
    chopped walnuts
1 teaspoon dried mint
2 tablespoons *kashk* paste

SERVES 6
as part of a mezze,
or as a starter

Preheat the oven to 400°F/200°C.

Peel the eggplants and cut them into equal-size small pieces, around 1¼ inches/3cm thick. Lay them across 2 rimmed baking sheets and drizzle with ¼ cup/60ml sunflower oil and 1 teaspoon salt. Use your hands to toss everything together to evenly coat, then bake for about 25 minutes until cooked through.

Heat 3 tablespoons sunflower oil in a large saucepan. Fry the onions for 25 minutes over medium-low heat until they are a deep brown (putting a lid on speeds things up a bit, just remember to keep checking them and stirring). If they start to look a bit dry, add a little more oil. Remove one-third of the onions from the pan and set aside.

Add the garlic to the pan and fry for a few minutes. Then add the eggplants, turmeric, mint, and lemon juice and mix well.

Add the just-boiled water, ½ teaspoon salt, a very generous grind of black pepper, and the *kashk* paste. Cover, lower the heat, and simmer for 15 minutes, stirring every so often so it doesn't catch, and mashing the eggplants with the back of your wooden spoon as you do so.

Meanwhile, prepare the toppings. Place 2 more tablespoons sunflower oil in a frying pan and add the reserved onions, frying them for a few more minutes over medium-high heat so they darken further and crisp up a bit. Then add the walnuts and dried mint and fry everything together for a couple of minutes until the walnuts turn glossy. Remove from the heat and set aside.

Continued on the next page

· ·

Now return to the eggplants. You'll need a bit of elbow grease to smash the mix into a thick, textured dip; I use a wooden spoon, but you can use a potato masher if you have one. It isn't supposed to be a purée—you want some texture—so a few lumps and bumps are fine. Taste to adjust the seasoning.

To serve, spread the warmed eggplant out on 2 flat or very shallow side plates. Mix the *kashk* paste for the topping with 1 tablespoon hot water to loosen it (you want the consistency of honey), then use this to decorate the plate. I make a cross of *kashk* paste and fill the quarters with the fried onion, walnut, and dried mint mixture.

Yogurt drink
AYRAN

This savory and salty yogurt drink is a hallmark of Turkish cuisine and I absolutely adore it. Versions of it are enjoyed throughout the Middle East and, in Iran, we often whisk in a teaspoon of dried spearmint, which is a particularly refreshing addition on a hot summer day. Ayran is especially tasty with grilled or fried meats, so make sure you try it with Adana kebabs or *Kuru köfte* (see pages 237 and 240).

2¼ cup/500g full-fat plain yogurt
1 quart/1 liter water
¾ teaspoon salt, or to taste
1 tablespoon dried mint (optional)

MAKES 6 SERVINGS

Place the yogurt, water, salt, and mint, if using, in a large saucepan or mixing bowl. Whisk the mixture with an immersion blender for around 30 seconds until there is a foam on top. Taste to see if you would like to add a pinch more salt.

Pour into a pitcher, then transfer to the refrigerator to chill for 1 hour before serving.

Yogurt with cucumber & mint

TZATZIKI/CACIK

This refreshing cucumber and yogurt appetizer is a staple of the Eastern Mediterranean kitchen. For an authentic taste, use strained Greek-style yogurt to make this recipe, as it has the requisite richness and creaminess that really sets a good version of the dish apart. You can also strain your own yogurt by buying a normal tub of Greek-style yogurt, spooning it into a cheesecloth, and straining it in a colander for a few hours until some of the water has drained off and it has a thick consistency. This makes a fantastic accompaniment to grilled meats.

7 oz/200g cucumber
1¾ cups/500g strained Greek-style
    yogurt
½ garlic clove, crushed
1 teaspoon dried mint
1 tablespoon finely chopped mint
    leaves or dill, plus more to serve
1 teaspoon lemon juice
2 tablespoons extra-virgin
    olive oil, plus more to serve
salt and black pepper

SERVES 4 TO 6
as part of a mezze

Slice the cucumber in half and use a small spoon to scoop out its seeds. Then grate it, place it in a colander over a plate to catch any water and sprinkle with ½ teaspoon salt. Let rest for 20 minutes, then use your hands to squeeze out excess water.

Place all the remaining ingredients in a bowl and then stir in the cucumber, adding a touch more salt and black pepper to taste. Finish with some fresh herbs and a slick of olive oil.

Turkish white beans

PİYAZ

I've eaten versions of this rustic, homely dish in tavernas in Athens, *meyhanes* in Istanbul, and seafront cafés in Cyprus. It is a subtle, delicious, and healthy plant-based main course or side dish. And because it is so simple, I'm not including a version of how you could make this with canned beans. Because even though you could, I want to encourage you to start cooking more with dried legumes, as the texture and flavor are so much better. As ever, the quality of olive oil is what will make or break this dish, so go for the best you can afford.

9 oz/250g dried white beans (I use Argentina white beans, but any will do)
3 tablespoons extra-virgin olive oil, plus more to serve
2 tablespoons lemon juice, or to taste
1½ garlic cloves, crushed
salt and black pepper

For the toppings
finely sliced red onion
finely chopped cilantro leaves
pul biber (Aleppo pepper), or sweet paprika

SERVES 4 TO 6
as part of a mezze

Rinse the beans, then soak them in a large bowl with plenty of cold water overnight.

The next day, drain the beans and place them in a large saucepan. Cover with enough just-boiled water to cover the beans by a couple of inches. Bring to a boil for 5 minutes, skimming off any scum that rises to the surface, then cover and simmer. Depending on the freshness of the beans, it will take anywhere between 25 and 45 minutes for them to soften.

When the beans are tender, drain and immediately dress them while they are still hot with the olive oil, lemon juice, garlic, 1½ teaspoons salt, and ½ teaspoon black pepper. Mix well and let rest for at least 15 minutes for the flavors to come together. Taste and adjust the seasoning to your preference; you may want a touch more salt or lemon juice.

To serve, drizzle with a couple more tablespoons of olive oil and top with very finely sliced red onion (I use a mandolin to slice this), cilantro, and a smattering of *pul biber* or paprika.

Almost fava

This is my version of a traditional Greek dish made from a variety of yellow split peas (called fava in Greek) that are blended and served warm with lots of lemon juice and olive oil. My version is adapted to use split mung beans instead, as they require minimal soaking and are easier to digest. You can find them in the "world food" section of larger supermarkets, natural food stores, or South Asian grocery stores. Of course, if you prefer to use fava, and can source those, go for it, though soak them for eight hours, or overnight, before you start.

I've eaten fava all over Greece, but my favorite version was in a café next to the central food market in Athens at one of those hole-in-the-wall places, unassuming and easy to walk past, hidden from street view and with no signs on the door, that lead you down crumbling steps to a dark and cool basement with wine barrels lining the walls. The owner, a portly older man in a white chef's jacket, didn't ask us what we wanted, but simply plonked the dish of the day down in front of us. Luckily it was a bowl of creamy fava, served with slices of tomatoes, onions, and cucumber, a hunk of bread, and a carafe of chilled white wine. It was the simplest of dishes and yet one of the most flavorsome and memorable of that trip.

As the ingredients are fairly minimal, be sure to use the best olive oil and vegetable stock that you can (I'm a fan of Marigold bouillon powder), and white pepper really makes a difference. Serve with some good bread, olives, tomatoes, cucumber, and some finely sliced onion.

For the fava
1¼ cups/250g yellow split mung beans
2 cups/480ml vegetable stock
1¾ cups/420ml just-boiled water
1 medium carrot, roughly chopped
1 medium onion, finely chopped
2 fat garlic cloves, crushed
2 bay leaves
2 thick thyme sprigs
finely grated zest of 1 large unwaxed
    lemon
3 tablespoons lemon juice
¼ cup/60ml extra-virgin olive oil
salt and white pepper

To serve
¼ small red onion, finely sliced
2 sweet, ripe tomatoes, in wedges
7 oz/200g cucumber, sliced into
    rounds
bread
olives
cilantro or parsley leaves, chopped
extra-virgin olive oil

SERVES 4
as part of a mezze,
or 2 to 3 as a main course

Rinse the mung beans and place them in a large bowl of cold water to soak for 20 minutes. Drain and transfer to a large saucepan. Add the stock and hot water, then bring to a boil for a couple of minutes, using a spoon to remove any scum that rises to the surface.

Add the carrot, onion, garlic, bay leaves, and thyme. Lower the heat, cover, and simmer for 30 to 40 minutes, until the beans are completely soft.

Discard the thyme and bay and stir in ¾ teaspoon salt and ¼ teaspoon white pepper. Add the lemon zest, lemon juice, and olive oil and cook for a further 5 minutes. Then remove from the heat and blend the contents of the pan, either by transferring the contents to a food processor or by using an immersion blender, until completely smooth. Taste and adjust the seasoning. You are looking for the consistency of hummus, so if you'd like it to be thicker, return to heat to evaporate the water for a few minutes (careful, it may splatter, so use a lid that is ajar). Alternatively, if it seems too thick, add a few more tablespoons of water.

Serve warm, with finely sliced onion, tomatoes, cucumber, and bread, olives, herbs, and a good drizzle of extra-virgin olive oil.

Smoky lima beans

GIGANTES PLAKI

This is one of those punchy pantry recipes that is easy to whip up as a midweek meal and takes its inspiration from a traditional Greek dish of beans baked in a tomato sauce. I make my version on the stove for speed, but you can transfer the beans to an oven-safe dish, cover with foil, and bake for 45 minutes at 350°F/180°C if you prefer. Lima beans have a creamier and meatier texture than other white beans, and they hold their shape better in longer cooking, making them perfect for slow-cooked stews. What gives this dish its unique flavor is the paprika (I add both the smoked and sweet versions, not the hot and spicy type), which adds a richness and earthiness that I find irresistible. I alternate between sprinkling crumbled feta on top of this dish and having it plain, as it's just as delicious without. Serve warm or at room temperature.

3 tablespoons vegetable oil
1 small onion, finely chopped
    (about 7 oz/200g)
2 garlic cloves, crushed
1 x 14.5-oz/400g can of diced plum
    tomatoes
1 teaspoon granulated sugar
1½ teaspoons dried oregano
1½ teaspoons sweet paprika
½ teaspoon smoked paprika
¼ teaspoon ground cinnamon
2 x 15-oz/425g cans of lima beans,
    drained and rinsed
¾ cup plus 2 tablespoons/200ml
    just-boiled water
3 tablespoons extra-virgin olive oil
1 tablespoon finely chopped dill,
    plus more to serve
1 tablespoon finely chopped
    parsley leaves, plus more
    to serve
⅔ cup/100g feta cheese, crumbled
    (optional)
salt and black pepper

SERVES 4
as part of a mezze,
or 2 to 3 as a main course

Heat the vegetable oil in a large saucepan. Add the onion and gently fry over medium heat for 12 to 15 minutes until soft. Add the garlic and cook for another few minutes, then add the tomatoes, sugar, oregano, both types of paprika, the cinnamon, 1 teaspoon salt, and a generous grind of black pepper. Cover and simmer for 15 minutes.

Add the beans to the tomato sauce with the hot water and another ½ teaspoon salt. Cover and cook over low heat for 30 minutes.

Stir in the extra-virgin olive oil and herbs and cook for a final 5 minutes. Taste, adjust the seasoning, and sprinkle with more herbs, and with crumbled feta if you fancy it, just before serving.

Afghan spiced pumpkin

BORANI KADOO

When I was in Lesvos, Afghans represented the largest group of refugees on the island and spending time with them gave me the opportunity to learn about their rich and diverse cuisine. Yogurt in savory dishes is one of the hallmarks of Afghan food; it's common to use it to cook vegetable and meat curries as well as to spoon dollops of it over braised vegetables or soups. Here the garlic-infused yogurt tops cubes of tangy and spicy sautéed pumpkin, which I like to serve with warm flatbreads, or alongside rice. Afghans like their food quite spicy, but I can't handle that I'm afraid, so this recipe is quite mild. Feel free to adjust the amount of heat by adding more chile to suit your taste.

For the pumpkin
1 medium pumpkin or butternut
    squash (around 2 lb 14 oz/1.3kg)
    peeled and chopped into
    1¼-inch/3cm cubes
2 tablespoons olive oil
salt and black pepper

For the spiced tomatoes
3 tablespoons sunflower oil
1 medium onion, finely chopped
2 garlic cloves, crushed
1¼-inch/3cm piece of ginger,
    peeled and finely chopped
1 green jalapeño, seeded and finely
    chopped
½ teaspoon cumin seeds
½ teaspoon coriander seeds
¼ teaspoon ground turmeric
4 ripe tomatoes (around 14 oz/400g),
    skinned (see page 59), seeded and
    chopped
½ teaspoon granulated sugar
7 tablespoons/100ml hot water
2 teaspoons dried mint, to serve

For the yogurt sauce
¾ cup plus 2 tablespoons/200g
    plain yogurt
¼ garlic clove, crushed

SERVES 4 TO 6
as part of a mezze

Preheat the oven to 375°F/190°C.

Place the pumpkin or squash on a baking sheet and toss with the oil and ¼ teaspoon salt. Transfer to the oven and roast for 25 to 30 minutes until cooked but still slightly firm.

To make the spiced tomatoes, heat the sunflower oil in a large pan and add the onion. Fry over medium heat for 15 minutes until it is soft. Add the garlic, ginger, and jalapeño and cook for 5 minutes. Toast the cumin and coriander seeds in a dry frying pan over medium heat for 1 minute or so until their aromas are released, then grind in a mortar and pestle and add to the pan with the turmeric, 1 teaspoon salt, and ¼ teaspoon black pepper. After the spices have cooked for a few minutes, add the tomatoes and sugar. Bring to a simmer, then cover and cook for 15 minutes.

Add the roasted pumpkin or squash and cook for 10 minutes, pouring in the hot water to loosen the sauce. Taste to adjust the seasoning.

Make the yogurt sauce by combining the yogurt, garlic, and ¼ teaspoon salt.

To serve, transfer the pumpkin or squash to a serving plate, spoon the yogurt sauce over the top, and sprinkle with the dried mint.

Stuffed roasted eggplants

İMAM BAYILDI

No one has ever been able to tell me exactly where the name of this eggplant dish comes from—translated it means "the imam fainted"—but its popularity is unquestionable across Turkey and the Levant. It's a great make-ahead dish as the flavors improve tremendously the next day. It may seem like there is a lot of oil going into this, but the eggplants need it to soak up the flavor, so don't scrimp. There may be some liquid in the roasting dish when the eggplants are removed from the oven, but as they cool this gets absorbed back, so just let them sit for a while. Serve at room temperature.

4 medium eggplants
    (total weight about 2⅔ lb/1.2kg)
extra-virgin olive oil
2 medium onions, finely chopped
3 tablespoons sunflower oil
2 teaspoons cumin seeds
4 fat garlic cloves, finely chopped
½ teaspoon sweet paprika
¼ teaspoon ground cinnamon
1 x 14.5-oz/400g can of diced plum
    tomatoes
1 teaspoon granulated sugar
2 teaspoons dried oregano
handful of parsley leaves, finely
    chopped, plus more
    to serve
salt and black pepper

SERVES 4 TO 6
as part of a mezze

Preheat the oven to 375°F/190°C.

Slice the eggplants in half and place in a roasting dish. Using a sharp knife, make 6 deep diagonal cuts into the flesh of each half (3 one way, then 3 across) without piercing the skin. Season with 1 teaspoon salt and a generous grind of black pepper

Brush the eggplants with 3 tablespoons extra-virgin olive oil and bake for 30 minutes or until completely soft.

Meanwhile, fry the onions in the sunflower oil for 20 minutes over low heat, until they have completely softened and browned.

Toast the cumin seeds by placing them in a dry frying pan over medium heat for a few minutes until their aroma is released. Then grind in a mortar and pestle and add to the onions with the garlic, paprika, cinnamon, 1 teaspoon salt, and a generous grind of black pepper. Fry for a few minutes before stirring in the tomatoes, sugar, and oregano. Simmer for 15 minutes, then add 2 tablespoons extra-virgin olive oil and the parsley and cook for a final 5 minutes.

When the eggplants are done, take the roasting dish out of the oven and, using a fork, mash the center of their flesh to create a well. Drizzle with 2 tablespoons extra-virgin olive oil and sprinkle with ½ teaspoon salt, then spoon on the tomato sauce, filling their centers and dotting any remaining sauce around. Cover the dish with foil and bake for 35 minutes, removing the foil for the final 10 minutes.

To serve, let the eggplants come to room temperature, sprinkle with some finely chopped parsley and, yes, a few more glugs of extra-virgin olive oil.

Broccolini with
red peppers & dill

Turkish cuisine features an array of vegetable dishes that are cooked simply, doused with olive oil, and served at room temperature. These dishes are called *zeytinyağlılar*, which means "those with olive oil," and this is my version of one made with Broccolini as I like the crunch and texture, though you could also substitute it with regular broccoli.

2 tablespoons vegetable oil
2 garlic cloves, finely sliced
1 medium red onion, sliced
    into half moons
1 large red bell pepper, roughly
    chopped into 1-inch/2.5cm
    pieces
1 teaspoon finely chopped dill
1 tablespoon lemon juice
½ teaspoon granulated sugar
9 oz/250g Broccolini,
    spears halved lengthwise
¼ cup/60ml water
extra-virgin olive oil
½ teaspoon *pul biber* (Aleppo
    pepper), or other mild
    chile flakes
salt and black pepper

SERVES 4
as a side dish,
or as part of a mezze

Place a saucepan over medium heat and pour in the vegetable oil. Add the garlic and fry for a couple of minutes, then add the red onion and stir well. Decrease the heat to low, cover with a lid, and cook for 4 to 5 minutes.

When the onion has softened, add the red bell pepper, dill, lemon juice, sugar, ¾ teaspoon salt, and a generous grind of black pepper. Stir again, cover, and cook for another 5 minutes.

Add the Broccolini along with the water. Cover and steam for about 4 minutes until it has just cooked through, but still has some bite.

Taste to adjust the seasoning, then transfer to a serving dish, drizzle with extra-virgin olive oil, and finish with a sprinkling of *pul biber* or other mild chile flakes.

Turkish braised carrots & leeks

ZEYTİNYAĞLI PIRASA

This comforting dish of braised vegetables, cooked in a slightly sweet-and-sour sauce, is a mainstay at the fast-casual restaurants in Turkey known as *lokantas*, which specialize in Turkish home-style cooking. The trick is to cook the leeks low and slow so they soften, sweeten, and caramelize. I like to use a wide sauté pan for this, to maximize the surface area for the vegetables. Serve it cold or at room temperature, with plenty of olive oil.

2 tablespoons vegetable oil
1 tablespoon salted butter
4 garlic cloves, finely sliced
2 to 3 leeks (total weight
　　about 1½ lb/700g), green bits
　　trimmed off, cut into
　　1-inch/2.5cm pieces
2 large carrots, cut into
　　½-inch/1cm diagonal pieces
3 tablespoons lemon juice,
　　or to taste
¾ teaspoon granulated sugar
½ cup plus 2 tablespoons/150ml
　　just-boiled water
1½ tablespoons finely
　　chopped dill
extra-virgin olive oil
salt and black pepper

SERVES 4
as a side dish or
4 to 6 as part of a mezze

Heat the vegetable oil in a large, wide pan over medium-low heat and add the butter. When it has melted, add the garlic and sauté for a few minutes.

Add the leeks and carrots, lemon juice, sugar, hot water, 1 teaspoon salt, and ½ teaspoon black pepper. Mix well, then place a lid on the pan. Cook over very low heat for about 45 minutes, stirring occasionally to make sure the leeks don't stick to the bottom.

After 45 minutes, check to make sure the leeks are fully soft. If so, add the dill and cook for 5 minutes. Turn off the heat and stir in 2 tablespoons of extra-virgin olive oil.

Let cool to room temperature, then check the seasoning, adding a touch more salt, pepper, or lemon juice to taste. Serve with several tablespoons of extra-virgin olive oil drizzled on top.

Halloumi saganaki

This is the perfect appetizer in my eyes: sweet, salty, crunchy, fried. Rectangles of halloumi are dusted in semolina or cornmeal, sautéed until crisp, drizzled with a warm, thyme-infused honey, and topped with crunchy pomegranate seeds. This recipe is inspired by a dish I kept returning to at the Loxandra restaurant in Nicosia, Cyprus and is one of the most popular mezze dishes that I make for my friends at home. Let's be honest, you can never go wrong with fried cheese. Enjoy!

10½ oz/300g halloumi cheese
1 large egg
¼ cup/40g fine semolina or cornmeal
3 tablespoons sunflower oil
2 tablespoons honey
1 teaspoon finely chopped thyme leaves
couple of handfuls of arugula leaves
4 to 5 fresh figs, quartered (optional)
3 tablespoons pomegranate seeds
black pepper

SERVES 4
as part of a mezze

Cut the halloumi into 8 thick slices.

Beat the egg in a small bowl and spread the semolina or cornmeal out on a plate. Dip the halloumi slices in the beaten egg, then roll them in the semolina or cornmeal so they have a crust around them.

Heat the oil in a nonstick frying pan until it is hot, then fry the halloumi pieces for a few minutes on each side until they are golden brown. Place on some paper towel to soak up any excess oil.

Meanwhile, heat the honey in a small saucepan with the thyme.

Now assemble the dish. Place the arugula on a serving plate and arrange the halloumi on top, nestling the figs around, if using. Drizzle a little of the hot honey over each slice of halloumi. Finish with a smattering of pomegranate seeds and grind some black pepper over the top.

Zucchini & feta fritters

MÜCVER

These herb-packed fritters make fantastic appetizers or even good sandwich fillers, popped into pockets of pita bread with some pickles and greens. They have the added bonus of being just as tasty at room temperature as they are when hot, so are useful to make ahead of time if you are having guests over, or to take on a picnic.

3 medium zucchini, grated (about
   1 lb 5 oz/600g)
4 green onions, finely chopped
3 garlic cloves, crushed
large handful of dill,
   finely chopped
large handful of parsley,
   finely chopped
1 teaspoon ground coriander
½ teaspoon sweet paprika
4 extra-large eggs, lightly beaten
finely grated zest of
   1 unwaxed lemon
½ cup/65g all-purpose flour
½ teaspoon baking powder
⅔ cup/125g feta cheese, crumbled
sunflower oil, for frying
salt and black pepper

MAKES ABOUT 16
SERVES 4 TO 6
as part of a mezze

Place the grated zucchini in a colander, either over a plate or in the kitchen sink, and sprinkle with 1 teaspoon salt, tossing the vegetables a little to make sure they are evenly coated. Set aside for 30 minutes for the salt to drain the water from the zucchini, then, using your hands, gently squeeze them to remove any excess water.

Place all the ingredients except the feta in a large bowl and beat well until thoroughly combined. Add ½ teaspoon salt and a generous grind of black pepper before gently folding in the crumbled feta.

In a large frying pan, heat 3 tablespoons oil over medium heat. When the oil is hot, spoon 1 heaped tablespoon of batter for each fritter into the pan. You'll need to cook these in batches, so as not to overcrowd the pan. Lightly press them down with the back of the spoon, flattening the fritters slightly, then cook for about 6 minutes, turning halfway, until cooked through, golden, and crisp on both sides.

Transfer to a paper towel–lined plate and keep warm while you cook the remaining fritters, adding more oil as necessary.

Charred cabbage with hazelnuts & chile butter

Here is a fun trivia night fact for you: Turkey is the world's leading producer of hazelnuts, growing around seventy-five percent of the world's supply in 600,000 farms scattered throughout its Black Sea region. Here, I've combined these sweet nuts with a sweet pointed cabbage, commonly called Hispi or sweetheart cabbage, which can be found in larger supermarkets or in Turkish or Asian grocery stores. I recommend using a griddle pan for this recipe, so you can get thick charred lines on the cabbage wedges, but it isn't strictly essential, you can just pop them in the oven and bake them if you want to skip that step.

1 large Hispi or sweetheart cabbage
    (about 1¾ lb/800g)
1 teaspoon cumin seeds
½ teaspoon coriander seeds
¼ teaspoon ground allspice
4 tablespoons/60ml olive oil
mounded ¼ cup/40g blanched
    hazelnuts, roughly chopped
3 tablespoons salted butter
½ teaspoon *pul biber* (Aleppo
    pepper), plus more to taste
handful of parsley leaves
salt and black pepper

SERVES 4
as a side dish

Preheat the oven to 400°F/200°C.

Cut the cabbage in half, keeping the stem intact, then cut each piece into thirds so you end up with 6 thick wedges. You'll get some random pieces falling off, but that's OK, you can transfer those bits straight to a rimmed baking sheet.

Place the cumin and coriander seeds in a dry pan over medium heat and toast them for 1 minute or so until their aromas are released. Grind the spices in a mortar and pestle and then mix in the allspice, oil, and ½ teaspoon salt. Spread this spiced oil over the cabbage, using your fingers to massage it into each piece.

Heat a griddle pan until it is very hot. Sear the wedges for about 4 minutes on each side until they are charred, then transfer to the baking sheet and roast for 20 to 25 minutes, or until the stalks are soft and tender.

Meanwhile, toast the hazelnuts in a dry pan over medium heat for a few minutes until they turn glossy and start to brown. Then add the butter and *pul biber*, lower the heat, and cook for a few minutes, stirring frequently to ensure the hazelnuts don't burn.

When the cabbage is ready, transfer it to a serving plate and spoon the chile butter and hazelnuts over the cabbage. Top with black pepper, a little more salt, the parsley, and a final smattering of *pul biber*.

Greek vegetable medley

This recipe is an adaptation of *briam*, a dish I ate frequently on the Greek island of Ikaria. It's a great way to use up a glut of seasonal vegetables and its simple flavoring relies on good-quality olive oil and slow, unhurried cooking. The flavors get better the next day, too, so it's a great make-ahead dish. In Greece, this is often served as a main course on its own, alongside some fresh bread and olives, but I like it with roast meats, grilled fish, or a bean stew.

2 large eggplants (total weight about 1¾ lb/800g)
olive oil
1 medium onion, finely chopped
3 fat garlic cloves, crushed
1 large potato (I use Cyprus potatoes), peeled and sliced into 1-inch/2.5cm thick pieces (12¼ oz/350g)
1 cup/240ml just-boiled water
2 cups/500g uncooked tomato purée
1½ teaspoons dried oregano
1 teaspoon dried thyme
1½ teaspoons sweet paprika
¼ teaspoon ground cinnamon
1 teaspoon granulated sugar
2 red bell peppers, sliced into 1½-inch/4cm chunks
1¼ cups/25g parsley leaves, finely chopped
salt and black pepper
extra-virgin olive oil, to serve

SERVES 4
as a side dish or
4 to 6 as part of a mezze

Preheat the oven to 400°F/200°C.

Slice the eggplants into 1½-inch/4cm thick pieces. Place them on a rimmed baking sheet (spread them over 2 sheets if they won't fit) and drizzle with ¼ cup/60ml regular olive oil and sprinkle with ½ teaspoon salt. Toss well to ensure they are well coated, then bake for 20 to 25 minutes until they have softened but are still quite firm. Keep the oven on, but lower the temperature to 325°F/170°C.

Heat 3 tablespoons more regular olive oil in a large saucepan. Add the onion and sauté for 10 minutes over medium-low heat. Add the garlic and fry for another couple of minutes. Then add the potato and hot water, cover, and simmer for 6 minutes.

Add the uncooked tomato purée, oregano, thyme, paprika, cinnamon, sugar, 1 teaspoon salt, and ½ teaspoon black pepper. Stir in the peppers and parsley, then gently fold in the roasted eggplants too.

Transfer all the vegetables to a large ovenproof dish, drizzle with another 3 tablespoons regular olive oil, cover with foil, and bake for 50 minutes.

Check all the vegetables are soft and cooked, then remove the foil and cook for a final 10 minutes.

Allow to cool slightly before serving, drizzled with extra-virgin olive oil.

Lentils with preserved lemons & zhoug

The inspiration for this recipe came from a conversation I had with a Yemeni refugee on the Greek island of Lesvos who had walked almost all the way from Yemen to Turkey to escape the war in his home country. This is an absolutely extraordinary feat by any standards, but even more so given he was injured from the war. We spoke about *oshaar*, a preserved lemon pickle, and *zhoug*, a spicy cilantro relish, both frequently used in Yemeni food, and it was these discussions that led me to create this dish. My version of *zhoug* is quite mild but, if you want to up the chile, feel free. The garlic in it is also quite intense if you eat it immediately, but the acidity mellows it out after an hour. Any leftover *zhoug* can be stored in the refrigerator for up to three days. To make this more substantial, I sometimes add a few halves of hard-boiled eggs. Serve at room temperature.

For the lentils
1 cup/200g green lentils
½ teaspoon cumin seeds
2 tablespoons lemon juice
4 tablespoons/60ml extra-virgin olive oil
3 heaped tablespoons finely chopped preserved lemon (rinsed before chopping)
7 oz/200g cooked beet, cut into 1-inch/2.5cm chunks
large handful of parsley leaves
salt and black pepper

For the zhoug
½ teaspoon cumin seeds
seeds from 1 green cardamom pod
1½ cups/30g cilantro leaves and stalks
1 cup/20g parsley leaves and stalks
1 green serrano chile, seeds and pith removed
1 large garlic clove
1 tablespoon lemon juice
3 tablespoons extra-virgin olive oil
2 tablespoons water
salt and black pepper

SERVES 2
as a main,
or 4 as part of a mezze

Rinse the lentils in cold water, then place them in a saucepan and cover with just-boiled water. Bring to a boil, then cover, lower the heat, and simmer for 15 to 20 minutes until they are soft but still have some bite. Depending on the age of your lentils, cooking times may vary.

To make the *zhoug*, toast the cumin and cardamom seeds in a dry frying pan over medium heat for 1 minute or so, until their aromas are released. Transfer to a mortar and pestle and crush the seeds. Then place them, along with all the other *zhoug* ingredients, in a small food processor and blitz with ¼ teaspoon each of salt and black pepper.

To assemble the dressing for the lentils, toast the cumin seeds in a small dry frying pan as before, then crush them in a mortar and pestle. When the lentils are ready, drain them in a sieve, return them to the pan and stir in the cumin, lemon juice, olive oil, preserved lemon, salt, and black pepper. It's important to do this while the lentils are still hot, as they soak up the flavors better. Stir in the beet and parsley and taste to adjust the seasoning.

Place the lentils in a shallow dish and spoon a few tablespoons of *zhoug* over and around, serving the rest on the side.

Sardines in grape leaves

Wrapping fish in grape leaves is a common cooking technique in the Eastern Mediterranean, as the leaves prevent the fish from burning and sticking to the barbecue. This is a great dish for when you are cooking outdoors, but also works well on a hot griddle pan. Just be sure to open a window and tutn on the vent if you are cooking these inside, as your kitchen will get smoky!

Sardines are an excellent choice of fish as they are both sustainable and highly nutritious, but their strong flavor demands they be as fresh as possible, so only make this if you can source very fresh fish. Get your nose right to it and give it a sniff: it shouldn't smell of anything but the sea. Also look for clear, glossy eyes, not sunken or bloodshot. Finally, sardines can really vary in size. I think smaller fish are tastiest, but if you find bigger sardines, just be aware that the bones will be quite large and you'll have to be a bit more careful eating them.

Eating the grape leaves is optional but I like the flavor they add.

For the dressing
2 garlic cloves, minced
6 tablespoons extra-virgin olive oil,
    plus more to fry if needed
5 tablespoons lemon juice
1 teaspoon finely grated
    unwaxed lemon zest
½ small hot red chile, seeded and
    finely chopped
small handful of parsley leaves
1½ tablespoons capers, rinsed
3 tablespoons finely chopped
    pitted green olives
salt

For the sardines
12 grape leaves, or as needed,
    depending on the size of
    the fish
12 fresh sardines, scaled and
    gutted but with heads on
    (these will be around 2 lb/900g
    total but can vary in size
    considerably, get enough for a
    couple for each guest)
3 tablespoons lemon juice
black pepper
lemon wedges, to serve

SERVES 4 TO 6
as part of a mezze

Begin by making the dressing. Place the garlic in a mortar and pestle and pound it with ½ teaspoon salt and 1 tablespoon of the oil until you get a thick paste. Spoon into a bowl with all the remaining dressing ingredients and mix well. Set aside for the flavors to infuse.

Rinse the grape leaves in cold water, then blanch them: place them in a large saucepan filled with boiling water and simmer for 5 minutes. Drain the leaves and refresh them by running them under cold water.

Season the fish with the lemon juice and a generous sprinkle of salt and black pepper both inside and outside.

Wrap each fish in 1 or 2 leaves (depending on their size), but allow their heads and tails to poke out.

As this point, you can either cook the sardines outside on a barbecue or cook them inside on a griddle pan over high heat (if you choose the latter, be sure to lightly brush the pan with some olive oil).

Grill each fish for about 3 minutes on each side. You can test to see if it is cooked by pulling a bit of flesh away; they are ready when it easily flakes off the bone. If the grape leaves start to burn, lower the heat.

Lay the fish on a serving plate and spoon on the dressing. Serve immediately with lemon wedges.

Pickled red cabbage

KIRMIZI LAHANA TURŞUSU

You'll do well to make yourself a jar of this sharp and crunchy pickle; it's easy to pull together and versatile too, so you can put it to good use on all manner of dishes. It's a fantastic accompaniment to grilled meats and fish (the acidity helps to cut through richness and fat) and I often add a few spoonfuls on top of salads, as it gives a gorgeous vibrant color and a welcome zing.

To get the cabbage sliced really finely, I use a mandolin on its middle setting (it's a piece of kitchen equipment that I really recommend buying), but you can, of course, just use a sharp knife. Just try to slice all the cabbage to the same thickness. You'll need to sterilize a large jar to store the cabbage in (see page 48).

1 lb 2 oz/500g (about ½ small) red cabbage, finely shredded
1 tablespoon salt
2 cups/480ml just-boiled water
½ cup plus 2 tablespoons/150ml white wine vinegar
1 teaspoon coriander seeds
½ teaspoon black peppercorns

MAKES ABOUT
12 SERVINGS

Place the shredded cabbage in a large bowl and sprinkle with the salt. Use your hands to massage the salt into the cabbage, then let it rest for 3 hours at room temperature (this draws out any bitter juices). Drain the cabbage in a colander and place it in a large sterilized jar.

Pour the boiled water and the vinegar into a saucepan, add the spices, and bring to a boil. Simmer for 3 to 4 minutes, then turn off the heat and let cool for 10 minutes.

Pour the infused vinegar over the cabbage. Seal the jar and allow it to pickle in a dark place for 3 days before serving. Once opened, store it in the refrigerator, where it will keep for about 1 month.

KITCHEN SPIRIT
LESVOS, GREECE

On a cobbled backstreet, down a dark, quiet lane in Mytilene, the largest city on the Greek island of Lesvos, there sits a restaurant called Nan.

Named after the word commonly used in Central Asia for "bread," Nan was founded by four Greek women with the aim of creating a social enterprise where Greek nationals and recent refugees to Lesvos could work together in a shared space. The goal was to create wealth for both parties, while fostering greater understanding between the two communities.

I visit Nan on my first night in Lesvos, walking away from the town's port—with its domineering European Border and Coast Guard Agency security ships waiting to patrol the seas and ensure that migrants don't cross—and turning into the labyrinth of side streets that occupy Mytilene's Old City. I have been drawn here initially by the restaurant's story, keen to do my bit to support an ethical social enterprise where refugees are able to earn a wage. But what keeps me coming back, night after night during my weeks on Lesvos, is the incredible food: a masterful blend of dishes from the Mediterranean, Middle East, and Indian subcontinent all served with that elusive, home-cooked feel.

I enjoy salads of arugula greens sweetened with wild mushrooms sautéed in butter, and smoky barbecued chicken marinated for several hours in yogurt and sweet paprika before hitting the kitchen's charcoal grill. Then there is the spiced red pepper and ground walnut dip, *muhammara*, which I scoop up with flatbreads and wash down with mint lemonade. But my favorite, perhaps, is the plump chickpea stew simmered with ginger, turmeric, and garam masala, a curry reminiscent of the food I grew up with and a dish cooked frequently by my Pakistani dad.

The atmosphere at Nan feels warm and convivial, almost as if you are in someone's home. The rickety wooden tables, made from the discarded pallets from cargo ships, are filled every night with groups of refugees, locals, or international NGO workers, all chatting loudly and animatedly over a global music soundtrack.

"We called it Nan because it is a word that anyone from Afghanistan, Iran, or Pakistan can understand," Lena Altinoglou, one of the owners of the restaurant, tells me, as she sits at one of the tables, inhaling thickly on her roll-up cigarette. "And like bread, we want to be the instrument that brings things together. Bread is a unifying part of a meal and we see ourselves as the unifying space in the island."

A schoolteacher by day, Lena spends her evenings and weekends running the restaurant and was one of its co-founders. She's a sprite-like figure, petite in size yet fierce in demeanor, constantly on the move: flitting between tables, taking orders, running errands, managing staff, and chatting to regulars as if they are members of her family. Over the years, it is clear that the restaurant has become an extension of her home, a social space in the community in which she gathers with those close to her.

"The idea was to set up a business where locals and refugees could work together, using their power, imagination and creativity. We wanted not only to integrate refugees into daily life on this island, but also help to restore their dignity, giving those who are in transit here the opportunity to earn their own money."

It takes several attempts to pin Lena down for a proper interview; each evening when I visit she scampers around the restaurant, barely catching her breath to talk with me for more than a few minutes. But one afternoon, before service starts, I join her for tea at the restaurant, to hear more about how it got started.

"These last few years have been very traumatic for the locals on this island, to have this refugee population here which is so utterly helpless and desperate," Lena says, pouring me a large cup of herbal tea infusion—I get wafts of saffron, orange, and cinnamon—from a china pot that sits in the middle of the table. "We had four years of a continuous flow of refugees. Four years of clashes and riots and protests. Half a million refugees crossed this island alone and we have a population of just forty thousand. Can you imagine that?" I shake my head; I can't.

"There were times that, wherever you went, you saw refugees sleeping in the port, in the parks, in the playground . . . every public space was occupied," Lena continues, the tempo of her words picking up speed. "You had NGOs going in and sharing food, water, blankets with refugees, but there was nowhere for people to put their waste, so the next day there were piles of garbage everywhere and no one to collect it."

"It sounds awful," I say, cringing inwardly at what little justice my reaction

does to the scene she describes. Lena nods, compassionately, and goes on, her voice rising as she speaks. "Then the Far Right started mobilizing and the discourse of hate and discrimination and racism started piling up and up and up." She pauses, and taps her cigarette on the ashtray. "It was from this space that we started Nan."

In 2016, following the dramatic rise in refugees fleeing conflicts and attempting to find safety in the West, the EU and Turkey signed an agreement to stop the flow of desperate people into Europe. As part of this, the EU had proposed paying the Turkish government €6 billion to keep refugees in Turkey and to help police the international waters that separate the Greek islands from the Turkish mainland, a stretch of water that—for Lesvos—is just three and a half nautical miles wide at its narrowest point.

Whether the full sum of money was paid (or was enough in the first place) has been hotly contested by the Turkish government, but nonetheless, the result of the agreement was that millions of refugees were granted settled status in Turkey. Any refugees that did manage to smuggle themselves to the Greek islands were no longer allowed to travel onward through Europe. While I am on Lesvos, it is clear that this has created a pressure-cooker situation, with tens of thousands of refugees trapped on the island, unable to leave the crowded and unsanitary camps in which they are held and, as a result, facing increased mental and physical health problems. It was against this backdrop that Lena and her friends decided to open a restaurant.

"We wanted this space to give a sense of solidarity and togetherness in the difficult situation everyone was dealing with. So when we designed the menu, we wanted it to be a mix of our local food, supporting Greek producers, with iconic recipes from Syria, Pakistan, or Afghanistan because that's where most of the refugees are coming from at the moment. Everyone who works here has contributed to the menu." She points to Abdul, a broad-shouldered Pakistani man, staunchly stationed at the grill, who is credited with devising the recipe for the exceptional chickpea stew (see page 209) that I keep ordering on my repeated visits. Then there is Waida, a plump, shy line cook with a dimpled smile, who makes the Syrian-inspired mezze dishes of smoky eggplant dips and beet and yogurt salads. Stratis, the only Greek man in the kitchen, came up with one of the restaurant's most popular dishes, chicken korma, which is served in the mildest manner, without any chile heat, so as to favor the Greek palate.

"The refugees on this island sometimes wait years to get the papers they need to leave and, in that time, you have to provide solutions for them,

solutions that are viable for everyone," Lena continues, as she chews on the walnut cookies she serves me with the tea. "The Europeans don't want these people, they would rather refugees stay out of sight, trapped on this island. So we have to make the best out of the situation, we have to show that the people of this island believe that refugees do have value and that we can build things together."

Struggling for words to match her determination, I tell her that, from my frequent visits to Nan, it's clear to me that she's achieved this purpose. The space has now evolved into something so much bigger than a restaurant; on an island that feels divided, it's a beacon of hope and inclusivity.

Lena nods as she starts gathering the plates and cups from our table. "My time on this island has taught me that we can't rely on the EU or our Greek government to solve all our problems," she says solemnly. "The only solutions will come from us, ordinary people, organizing as a community and showing we can work together, eat together, feed each other, and grow together." She carries our used crockery over to the kitchen counter, then turns to me, smiling. "In my eyes, the Greek people have much they can learn from refugees who come here, and the refugees have much to learn from Greek people. Our governments might try to tell us we are different, but being here, talking to people, working with them, and eating with them, all I see is our similarity."

SALADS

There's no dish that epitomizes Eastern Mediterranean food more than a salad. And by that, of course, I mean the most famous salad of the region: the Greek salad. The marriage of sweet tomatoes and tangy sheep cheese is a flavor combination so perfect that I'm surprised it's not mentioned in one of the ancient Greek myths. For some reason, the best versions are often eaten under a beach umbrella, with wet hair and the taste of salt water still lingering faintly on your lips.

One afternoon on the Greek island of Ikaria, I watched a waiter carry one such salad in a large shallow bowl over to where I was sitting. One of his hands was entrusted with the hefty dish, topped with a slab of creamy white feta the size of my palm, and the other held a small caddy with bottles of olive oil and red wine vinegar. He left me to dress the salad myself, drizzling the oil and vinegar over the top, before ferociously tapping the salt mill on the side of my table to dislodge its humidified solid contents. The end result was perfect: triangular chunks of warm tomatoes and chilled cucumbers dotted with black olives and thin rings of crisp red onion, all brought together with the rich salty cheese. Of course, Greek salad isn't the only salad you'll find in this part of the world, but when it's done well, it's probably one of the best.

. . . .

The Greeks, Turks, and Cypriots are united in their affection for freshly chopped raw vegetables, which appear at almost every meal. They are either assembled into salads, or cut simply into thick slices to accompany dishes. I've included some of my favorite regional specialties here, but also some salads inspired by ingredients I like to buy at local markets on my trips. I've tried to include salads for every season, too, so you can enjoy them all year round.

Greek salad

If there's one dish that conjures up images of the Greek islands for me, it is this, the classic Greek salad. In all honesty, it is best enjoyed when looking out at the Mediterranean Sea with sand between your toes, but on a hot summer's day its sweet and salty flavors can be refreshing and delicious wherever you are. As with all simple dishes, it helps to pay attention to a few key details to get it just right. So make sure your tomatoes are sweet, ripe, and juicy, keep the cucumber in the refrigerator until just before serving (this salad needs to be cold to be refreshing) and don't crumble the cheese, serve it in a thick slice as they do in Greece. I like to keep the tomato and cucumber pieces quite chunky and large, as I prefer the aesthetic and it is how it's traditionally served. If you find raw onions a bit pungent for your taste, you can marinate them in the salad dressing before assembling; this will soften them and remove some of their astringency. Serve with plenty of crusty bread to soak up the juices.

For the dressing
2 tablespoons extra-virgin olive oil, plus more to serve
1 tablespoon lemon juice
1 tablespoon red wine vinegar
salt and black pepper

For the salad
½ small red onion, finely sliced, or to taste
4 medium-size ripe tomatoes (total weight about 1 lb 2 oz/500g)
1 lb 2 oz/500g cucumber
handful of Kalamata olives
1 tablespoon capers, rinsed
⅓ green bell pepper, cut crosswise into 3 circles
5¼oz/150g feta cheese
1 teaspoon dried oregano

SERVES 4
as a side dish, 2 as a main

Start by making the dressing, whisking all the ingredients together in a bowl with ½ teaspoon salt and ¼ teaspoon black pepper. (If you want to marinate the onion first, add it to the dressing now, letting it soften there for 20 minutes.)

Cut the tomatoes into large, thick, wedges, about ¾ inch/2cm wide. Peel the cucumber and cut it into thick, diagonal slices about ¾ inch/2cm wide also, then cut these slices in half, so they are roughly the same size as the tomatoes.

Place the tomatoes, cucumber, and onion in a large bowl. Add the dressing and toss together well.

Scatter the olives and capers over the salad, layer on the slices of green bell pepper, and place a large piece of feta on top. Drizzle the entire salad with a bit more extra-virgin olive oil and finish with the dried oregano.

Turkish shepherd's salad

ÇOBAN SALATASI

Variations of this crisp and refreshing salad appear across Eastern Mediterranean and Middle Eastern kitchens, where they are an essential accompaniment to most meals. This really is a staple of the region, which is why I make no apologies for having similar versions of it in each of my books. When you are cutting vegetables, the aim is to have an equal ratio of tomato to cucumber, so let that be your guide more than the quantities given below. Also, be sure to cut the tomatoes and cucumber into same-size pieces for uniformity of texture. And be generous with the lemon juice in the dressing—this is supposed to be sharp!

4 medium Persian cucumbers,
    or 1 lb 2 oz/500g regular
    cucumbers
4 medium tomatoes
1 Turkish long green pepper,
    or 1 regular green bell pepper
¼ red onion
large handful of parsley leaves,
    finely chopped
3 tablespoons extra-virgin olive oil
3 tablespoons lemon juice,
    or to taste
sumac (optional)
salt and black pepper

SERVES 4
as a side dish

Slice the cucumbers in half and use a small spoon to scoop out and discard their watery seeds. Chop them into 1-inch/2.5cm chunks.

Quarter the tomatoes, scoop their seeds out, and slice them into pieces that are roughly the same size as the cucumbers.

Chop the green pepper and red onion into slightly smaller pieces than the other vegetables (around ½ inch/1cm), then place all the vegetables in a large bowl.

Dress the salad with the chopped parsley, oil, lemon juice, ½ teaspoon salt, and ¼ teaspoon black pepper. Taste and adjust the seasoning to your taste; this is supposed to be sharp, so add more lemon juice if necessary, and top with a good sprinkle of sumac if you have any around.

Sweet potato, chickpea, & tahini salad

This is the kind of food I most enjoy eating: chunky roasted vegetables, garlicky tahini sauce, lots of herbs, lots of citrus. You can't go wrong. I use chickpeas in jars for this recipe, as they are softer and I can find them easily and affordably in my local Turkish greengrocer. As these might not be available to you, I've suggested using canned chickpeas here instead (though if you can find the type in jars I highly recommend it). Brands of cans vary massively, so you may need to cook them for a little longer until they are soft.

For the sweet potatoes
1 lb 10 oz/750g orange-fleshed
   sweet potatoes
2 tablespoons olive oil
1 teaspoon fennel seeds
1 teaspoon dried thyme
salt and black pepper

For the chickpeas
1½ teaspoons cumin seeds
2 tablespoons olive oil
1 garlic clove, minced
2 x 15-oz/425g cans of chickpeas,
   drained and rinsed
2 tablespoons lemon juice
½ cup/120ml just-boiled water

For the tahini sauce
¼ cup/80g tahini
¼ cup/60ml water, or as needed
2 tablespoons lemon juice

For the rest
2 Little Gem lettuces,
   roughly chopped
2 handfuls of parsley leaves,
   finely chopped
2 tablespoons pumpkin seeds
¾ cup/125g feta cheese, crumbled
   (optional)
1 to 2 teaspoons sumac

SERVES 4 TO 6
as part of a mezze or side dish,
or 2 to 3 as a main course with bread

Preheat the oven to 400°F/200°C.

Peel the sweet potatoes and cut them into 1½-inch/4cm chunks. Place them on a rimmed baking sheet, drizzle with the olive oil, and sprinkle with the fennel seeds, thyme, and ½ teaspoon each of salt and black pepper. Toss well to ensure the vegetables are properly coated, then bake for 20 minutes until soft. Remove from the oven and let them cool on the sheet.

Meanwhile, prepare the chickpeas. Begin by toasting the cumin seeds in a dry frying pan over medium heat for 1 minute or so, until their aromas are released, then crush them in a mortar and pestle.

Heat the olive oil in a saucepan over medium heat, add the cumin and garlic, and stir gently. Fry for 1 minute or so, then add the chickpeas, lemon juice, just-boiled water, 1 teaspoon salt, and ½ teaspoon black pepper. Lower the heat, cover, and cook for 10 to 15 minutes, or until the chickpeas have softened. Then remove the lid and increase the heat for a few minutes to evaporate any liquid from the pan. Set aside and let cool.

To make the tahini sauce, place all the ingredients in a small bowl with ¼ teaspoon each salt and black pepper and mix with a fork. Taste and adjust the seasoning. You may need to add a touch more water if your tahini is very thick; you are looking for a sauce that is the consistency of honey.

Assemble the dish by placing the lettuces, parsley, chickpeas, and sweet potatoes in a large serving bowl. Drizzle the tahini sauce and toss everything together well. Top with the pumpkin seeds and crumbled feta, if using, then finish with a generous sprinkling of sumac and black pepper.

Cypriot potato salad

A zesty, herb-packed potato salad, perfect for serving alongside grilled meats or fish. Try to use Kalamata olives here, but, if you can't find those, just aim for the olives to be oily rather than briny in these dishes. I don't know what it is about Cyprus potatoes that makes them taste so extraordinarily good, but if you can find any of these flavorsome spuds you won't be disappointed. If not, any waxy or new potatoes will do. Just be sure to toss the dressing in while the potatoes are still warm, as they absorb the flavors better.

2 lb 2 oz/1kg Cyprus or new
   potatoes
finely grated zest of 1 medium
   unwaxed lemon
¼ red onion, finely sliced
⅓ cup/60g black olives, pitted and
   roughly chopped
2 tablespoons capers,
   drained and rinsed
handful of mint leaves,
   finely chopped
handful of cilantro,
   finely chopped
1 teaspoon dried oregano
3 tablespoons extra-virgin olive oil
2 tablespoons lemon juice
salt and black pepper

SERVES 4

Cut the potatoes into large (2-inch/5cm) chunks. I like to leave the skins on, but remove them if you prefer.

Bring a large saucepan of water to a boil. Add 1 teaspoon salt and the potatoes to the pot and boil for about 12 minutes until they are soft. Drain and place in a serving bowl.

Add all the remaining ingredients along with ¼ teaspoon salt and a generous grind of black pepper.

Spicy bulgur in lettuce cups

KISIR

If, like me, you relish food that you can eat with your hands, you'll take great pleasure in assembling and eating these salad wraps. Originating from the southeast of Turkey, where pomegranate molasses is used to add a sweet-and-sour piquancy to food, this dish can be served from a large salad bowl, or you can nestle scoops of it inside lettuce leaves which, in my opinion, brings a bit of glamour to the party. Traditionally a hot pepper paste known as *biber salçası* is added to kısır; you can find it in Turkish grocery stores or online. It isn't strictly essential, though, and you can always adjust the heat levels to your taste with chile flakes. Serve as part of a mezze spread or alongside grilled meats or fish.

1 cup/200g fine bulgur wheat
1½ cups/350ml just-boiled water
3 green onions, finely chopped
3 ripe tomatoes,
    very finely chopped
1 small Persian cucumber,
    very finely chopped (about
    3½ oz/100g)
large handful of parsley
    leaves, finely chopped
small handful of mint leaves,
    finely chopped
½ cup/50g walnuts
seeds of ½ medium pomegranate
2 baby romaine or Little Gem
    lettuces, leaves separated
    (optional)

For the dressing
5 tablespoons extra-virgin olive oil
3 tablespoons pomegranate
    molasses, or to taste
3 tablespoons lemon juice,
    or to taste
1½ tablespoons tomato paste
½ to 1 teaspoon *pul biber*
    (Aleppo pepper), or to taste
1 teaspoon *biber salçası* (Turkish
    hot pepper paste, optional)
salt and black pepper

SERVES 4 TO 6
as part of a mezze

Place the bulgur in a large bowl and pour in the just-boiled water. Stir briskly, cover with a plate, and let steam for 10 minutes for the grains to soften.

Make the dressing by whisking all the ingredients together with 1 teaspoon salt and ½ teaspoon black pepper. Once the grains have absorbed the water, pour in the dressing and stir well to combine. Add the green onions, tomatoes, cucumber, and herbs.

Heat a small dry frying pan over medium heat and tip in the walnuts, toasting them lightly for 1 minute or so until they turn glossy. Transfer to a chopping board, finely chop them, then add to the salad.

Finally add the pomegranate seeds and mix everything together. Taste to adjust the seasoning (you may want to play around with the levels of pomegranate molasses, lemon juice, heat, and salt), then spoon into the lettuce leaves, if you like, and arrange on a large platter, or serve from the bowl as it is.

Tomato & za'atar salad

All over the Eastern Mediterranean tomatoes are a prized ingredient, sweet and sun-kissed, needing just a sprinkle of salt to be enjoyed as a delicious snack. Here, I've combined them with a za'atar herb mixture and a sweet-and-sour red wine vinegar dressing for what I believe to be the perfect summer tomato salad. Use whatever tomatoes you prefer—I like a variety of plum, heirloom, and cherry—just make sure they are as ripe and sweet as possible. To optimize their flavor, don't keep tomatoes in the refrigerator, as the cold deadens it. If you want a little hack, if my tomatoes feel a bit underripe, I sometimes leave them in the sun for a few hours; it does seem to make them taste sweeter.

For the dressing
3 tablespoons extra-virgin olive oil
2 tablespoons red wine vinegar
1 teaspoon honey
½ teaspoon finely grated
    unwaxed lemon zest
1½ tablespoons za'atar
salt and black pepper

For the salad
1¾ lb/800g variety of sweet and
    ripe plum, heirloom, and
    cherry tomatoes
¼ red onion, finely sliced
    (I like rings or half-moons)
2 tablespoons capers,
    drained and rinsed
handful of black olives
handful of basil leaves,
    roughly torn
pul biber (Aleppo pepper),
    to serve (optional)

SERVES 4 TO 6
as a side or as part of a mezze

Whisk all the dressing ingredients together with ½ teaspoon salt and ¼ teaspoon black pepper.

Roughly chop the tomatoes into 1½-inch/4cm chunks, playing around with the sizes of the different fruits for a variety of textures, then place in a salad bowl.

Scatter the onion, capers, and olives around the tomatoes, then pour the dressing over the top and toss well.

Add the torn basil leaves, toss again, and finish with a sprinkle of *pul biber*, if you like.

Sunshine salad

This cheerful salad is inspired by the magnificent bounty of Cyprus's late summer produce and—I really make no apologies for this cliché—looks and tastes like sunshine on a plate. Avocados grow in the west of the island, in its unique subtropical microclimate, and the creamy fruit pairs especially well with halloumi, the island's (and everyone else's) favorite squeaky cheese.

For the salad
3 medium-size sweet potatoes
    (total weight about 2⅔ lb/1.2kg)
2 tablespoons olive oil
2 large handfuls of arugula
6⅓ oz/180g cherry tomatoes
    (16 to 18), halved
1 large ripe Hass avocado, peeled,
    stoned, and sliced
small handful of mint leaves,
    finely chopped
small handful of basil leaves,
    finely chopped
9 oz/250g halloumi cheese
vegetable oil
salt and black pepper

For the dressing
3 tablespoons extra-virgin
    olive oil
1½ tablespoons apple
    cider vinegar
½ teaspoon finely grated
    unwaxed lemon zest

SERVES 4 TO 6
as a side dish, or 3 as a main course
with some bread

Preheat the oven to 400°F/200°C.

Peel the sweet potatoes and slice into wedges that are roughly 1¼ inches/3cm thick and 2½ inches/6cm long. Place them on a baking sheet and drizzle with the olive oil, ½ teaspoon salt, and a generous grind of black pepper. Transfer to the oven and bake for around 30 minutes, or until they are cooked but still firm.

Place all the dressing ingredients in a bowl with ½ teaspoon salt and ¼ teaspoon black pepper and whisk together.

Once the sweet potatoes are cooked, let them cool on the sheet before putting them in a large serving bowl along with the arugula, tomatoes, avocado, and herbs. Drizzle the dressing over the salad and toss well to ensure everything is well combined.

Slice the halloumi into 8 rectangular pieces and heat some vegetable oil in a frying pan over medium-high heat. Fry the halloumi for a couple of minutes on each side until golden and seared, then arrange it on top of the salad. Serve immediately.

Grilled onion salad with pomegranate & sumac

This zippy salad is an essential accompaniment to grilled meats at the Turkish restaurants in the area of Northeast London where I live, and I sometimes wonder if I order the kebabs just to get a side of this. You can cook the onions on a barbecue, or on a griddle pan on the stove. In Hackney, this recipe is made with şalgam suyu, a fermented carrot and turnip juice, which you can find in any Turkish grocery store or online. However, as that might prove a bit hard to track down, I've substituted a couple of spoons of sour and salty gherkin pickle juice. It may seem like a lot of dressing initially but fear not, you'll definitely want to mop it up with your flatbread and I've been known to drink it from a spoon. To get the sweet and sourness you're after here, tinker a bit and add more sour if you want.

2 medium white onions,
    peeled and cut into 6 wedges
    (total weight about 1 lb/450g)
extra-virgin olive oil
3 tablespoons pomegranate
    molasses, or to taste
3 tablespoons şalgam suyu
    juice, gherkin juice, or any
    other pickle juice, or to taste
1 teaspoon pul biber
    (Aleppo pepper)
2 teaspoons sumac
3 tablespoons water
2 tablespoons lime juice,
    or to taste
handful of parsley leaves,
    finely chopped
handful of mint leaves,
    finely chopped
salt and black pepper

SERVES 4 TO 6

Toss the onion wedges in a little olive oil and ½ teaspoon salt. If you are cooking over a barbecue, thread the onions on skewers and cook for about 10 minutes, turning every few minutes, until they are soft and charred. If you are cooking these inside, heat a griddle pan until it's very hot and then grill the onions on both sides and on their backs until they are cooked through. They may take a little longer if cooking on the stove, 12 to 15 minutes, depending on your pan. When the onions are ready, transfer them to a salad bowl and let cool for a few minutes.

Make the dressing by whisking together the pomegranate molasses, pickle juice, pul biber, sumac, water, lime juice, and 2 tablespoons olive oil, along with ½ teaspoon salt and a generous grind of black pepper. Pour this over the onions, add the herbs, and toss everything together.

Taste to adjust the seasoning, adding a touch more salt, pomegranate molasses, lime juice, or pickle juice to your preference. This will happily sit for a few hours, or you can serve it straight away.

For recipe photo, see page 239

Arugula, mushroom, & kefalotyri salad

This warm salad was a revelation when I had it at Nan, a restaurant on the Greek island of Lesvos (see page 137). Wild mushrooms create a rich umami flavor that marries well with the hard and salty cheese and the peppery olive oil for a simple yet delicious side salad that is really good alongside a hearty roasted chicken or a moussaka (see page 210). *Kefalotyri* is a hard and salty Greek cheese made from a mix of sheep and goat milk. You can sometimes find it in specialty cheese shops, but Parmesan also works as a substitute if that is more accessible to you.

5¼ oz/150g arugula
2 tablespoons salted butter
1 lb 3 oz/550g mixed mushrooms (brown button, oyster, and shiitake, for instance), roughly sliced into equal-size shapes
½ teaspoon dried oregano
4 teaspoons red wine vinegar, or to taste
extra-virgin olive oil
about ¾ oz/20g shavings of *kefalotyri* or Parmesan cheese
salt and black pepper

SERVES 4

Place the arugula in a serving bowl.

Melt the butter in a large saucepan over medium heat. Add the mushrooms, stir well to coat them in the butter, then sprinkle with the oregano, some salt, and a generous grind of black pepper. Cook for 7 to 10 minutes over medium-high heat until the mushrooms have softened but still have some bite. You want to keep the heat quite high so the mushrooms don't end up sitting in their own juices. When they are done, take the pan off the heat, add 2 teaspoons of the red wine vinegar, and let cool for 10 minutes.

Toss the mushrooms with the arugula, adding the remaining 2 teaspoons red wine vinegar and 1 tablespoon extra-virgin olive oil. Taste to adjust the seasoning (you may want a bit more vinegar or salt), then top with the cheese (I use a vegetable peeler to shave off very thin shards and scatter them over the salad). Finish with a final drizzle of extra-virgin olive oil.

Crunchy winter slaw

This salad utilitizes the humble turnip, surely one of the world's most underrated vegetables. In Turkey, I was introduced to eating turnips raw for the first time, as they are often served in small wedges as an accompaniment to soup. I was absolutely enamored with their sweet flavor and crunchy texture and have found they work really well in salads, so in this recipe I've paired them with carrots and cilantro for a healthy winter slaw.

For the slaw
5¼ oz/150g turnips, cut into fine,
    equal-size matchsticks
5¼ oz/150g carrots, cut into fine,
    equal-size matchsticks
¼ small red cabbage, finely
    shredded (about 7 oz/200g)
handful of cilantro leaves, roughly
    chopped (or substitute arugula if
    you prefer)

For the dressing
3 tablespoons extra-virgin
    olive oil
1 tablespoon apple cider
    vinegar, or to taste
1 tablespoon lemon juice,
    or to taste
finely grated zest of
    1 unwaxed lemon
1 teaspoon honey
1 teaspoon poppy seeds
salt and black pepper

SERVES 4

Prepare all the vegetables and herbs and place them in a bowl. I use a mandolin for the cabbage as I find it the easiest way to produce very fine, equal slices.

Place all the dressing ingredients in a bowl and season with ½ teaspoon salt and ¼ teaspoon black pepper. Use a fork to whisk everything together. Pour the dressing over the salad and mix well. Taste and adjust the seasoning. You may want a touch more acidity in the form of lemon juice or vinegar, or a little extra salt, or both.

You can serve this immediately, but it will also happily sit for 1 hour or so if you want to make it ahead of time.

Beet, fennel, & pomegranate salad

Cold beet salads are served all over Greece and this was inspired by the many that I've enjoyed in tavernas and restaurants. My version has a bit more bite to it, combining the sweet beet with juicy green apples, pomegranate seeds, and thin strips of fennel for a sweet and crunchy dish. For ease and speed, I use the pre-cooked vacuum-packed beet you can buy in supermarkets and grocery stores but, of course, you can use freshly cooked beets if you prefer. Simply wrap the beets in foil and bake for around forty-five minutes in an oven preheated to 400°F/200°C until they are soft. If you are using the store-bought variety, just make sure that they are plain, not pickled in vinegar.

This is one of those dishes that works best when you slice the ingredients with a mandolin and, as this is quite an affordable kitchen tool, I highly recommend getting one.

For the salad
12¼ oz/350g cooked beet
1 green apple
1 medium fennel bulb (about 9 oz/250g)
large handful of parsley leaves and stalks, finely chopped
small handful of mint leaves, finely chopped
2 tablespoons finely chopped dill
⅔ cup/120g pomegranate seeds

For the dressing
3 tablespoons pomegranate molasses
2 tablespoons lemon juice
3 tablespoons extra-virgin olive oil
salt and black pepper

SERVES 4 TO 6

Slice the beet into 1¼-inch/3cm pieces and place in a serving bowl. (You may want to wear gloves while you do this, as beet stains your fingers.)

Use a mandolin or a large, sharp knife to thinly slice the apple and fennel, avoiding the core of the fennel bulb. I use the middle setting on my mandolin, which makes them ⅛-inch/3mm thick.

Add the apple, fennel, herbs, and pomegranate seeds to the salad bowl, then pour in the dressing ingredients, along with ½ teaspoon salt and ¼ teaspoon black pepper.

Toss the salad well to ensure the ingredients are fully coated with the dressing, then taste to adjust the seasoning.

Ezme salad

Sitting somewhere between a salad and a salsa, ezme is a popular mezze dish originating in Eastern Turkey, near the Syrian border. Like many of the dishes from that region, it's flavored with generous amounts of pomegranate molasses, sumac, and *pul biber*, creating a delicious sweet, sour, and spicy flavor combination that is incredibly addictive. *Ezme* can be translated as "to crush" or "to mash" and that's exactly what the texture of this dish feels like. Feel free to adjust the heat levels to your preference by adding a bit more chile if you like. Either serve it with some *lavaash* bread to scoop it up, or as a side dish to grilled meats or fish. The spinach leaves aren't authentic, but I find they add a welcome texture and flavor, so I like to throw them in to bulk it up a bit. (It's also not terribly authentic to serve this with tortilla chips but, to be honest, I've been known to do it and think that it's a winner.)

For the salad
6 ripe tomatoes (total
    weight about 1 lb 7 oz/650g)
2 Turkish long green peppers,
    or ½ regular green bell pepper
    (around 3 oz/80g)
½ small onion (3½ oz/100g)
1 garlic clove, crushed
¼ cup/5g mint leaves, finely
    chopped
¾ cup/15g parsley, finely chopped
3½ oz/100g spinach leaves, finely
    chopped (optional)

For the dressing
2 tablespoons pomegranate
    molasses, or to taste
2 tablespoons extra-virgin
    olive oil, plus more to serve
1 tablespoon lemon juice
1 teaspoon *pul biber* (Aleppo
    pepper), or to taste
1 teaspoon sumac
salt and black pepper

SERVES 4 TO 6

Peel the tomatoes (see page 59), halve them, and remove the seeds, then chop them as small as you can, aiming for equal-size shapes of around ¼ inch/5mm. Place them in a serving bowl.

Halve the green peppers, remove the seeds and pith, chop into similar-size tiny pieces, and add them to the tomatoes. Cut the onion into similar-size pieces, too, and add it with the garlic.

Add the finely chopped herbs and spinach, if using, then examine your dish. If it looks like it needs it, re-chop some of the ingredients so they are uniformly diced.

Mix all the dressing ingredients in a bowl with ½ teaspoon salt and ¼ teaspoon black pepper and pour it over the salad. Toss well, then taste to adjust the seasoning. Let the salad marinate for 30 minutes before serving, then taste again and add a squeeze more pomegranate molasses or *pul biber* if you want some added punch. Top with a drizzle of olive oil just before serving.

HOME FOR A DAY
LESVOS, GREECE

Lesvos is Greece's third largest island, situated in the Aegean Sea just sixteen miles from Turkey. It's a breathtakingly beautiful place, with long stretches of sandy beaches next to crystal-clear waters, thickly forested mountains with therapeutic hot springs, salt marshes that are home to flamingos and wild birds, and more than eleven million olive trees (yes really) that are cultivated for the island's most important food product: olive oil.

But amid all its beauty, Lesvos carries a heavy load. For in recent years, this island—once a major tourist attraction—has taken on a more troubling story. Its proximity to Turkey has made it the first stop for many refugees en route to Europe, who arrive by boat after a perilous journey by land and sea.

One afternoon in early 2014 a local fisherman, Nikos Katsouris, came across a large group of refugees who had just landed on the shore. Shocked at their story of fleeing the war in Syria and the journey that had brought them to this quiet, sleepy island, he felt moved to help them, buying them food to eat and giving them whatever spare clothes he had with him. Later, when he arrived home, he told his wife Katerina what he had seen and, as soon as she heard the story, she threw herself into the kitchen, preparing home-cooked meals to take to them. Hours later, the couple filled their car with food and every blanket and spare item of clothing they could grab and went to the area where Nikos had seen the newcomers. Unable to find them, after much searching, eventually they learned that the refugees had been detained by the local police and upon heading to the police station (and despite their best efforts) neither Nikos or Katerina—nor their food—were allowed in.

Stunned by the day's dramatic events, the couple drove back to the beach, a place where they often went to reflect. There they began to consider a situation that—though they didn't know it at the time—was emerging in Lesvos and throughout the region, where more boats kept on arriving. They stayed, talking until nightfall, when all of a sudden they heard voices coming from the water. After several minutes, an inflatable dinghy came bobbing its way toward the shore, filled with cold, scared, soaking wet people.

It was a great surprise to everyone on the boat to find a couple sitting on the beach, seemingly waiting for them and able to provide blankets, clothes, and home-cooked meals. "This," Katerina tells me, "is how it all started."

In the months and years that followed, more and more refugees kept arriving on Lesvos, and Nikos and Katerina continued to feed them. First, they worked with other volunteers and made meals to deliver to the refugee camps. Later, at their small fish restaurant, they would serve refugees free meals and allow them to take up seats alongside paying customers from the local community. But, as the years went on, the situation on Lesvos intensified, both in terms of swelling numbers of refugees and increased conflict with locals. Eventually, Nikos and Katerina made the decision to shut their business completely and transition their space into operating as a non-profit restaurant, serviced by volunteers, that served free meals every day to the residents of the refugee camps.

"I have a philosophy about cooking," Katerina tells me, as I visit their restaurant, which they have called Home For All. "Cooking for me is an art and it is a philosophy. If you don't eat, you will die. So giving food is like giving life. And I want to help people live."

Home for All is situated on the banks of a fishing port on the edge of the Gulf of Yera, a deep inlet of sea in the center of the island. Each day a volunteer drives a minivan to one of the camps and, over several round trips, brings around forty refugees to the restaurant. Over the course of a few hours, people talk, kids play, groups sing or play music, and everyone is served a meal, on tables with white linen, with ceramic plates and glassware.

On my first visit I join Katerina around 1 pm, just before the first group of refugees arrive from the notorious Moria camp, where violence is high, sexual assault common, and stabbings regular occurrences. On the week I arrive in Lesvos, Doctors Without Borders reported that the situation was so dire that children as young as ten were attempting suicide in camps. "If I'd known it would have been this bad here, I wouldn't have come," a young Iranian from Tehran tells me forlornly. He's not the first or last person to say this to me.

The stories of the people I have met during the week swirl around my head as I wait for lunch to be prepared. I think of Kamara, the fitness instructor from Libera; Dadar, the Kurdish librarian at One Happy Family; Farnaz, the Afghan carpenter; Sajaad, the Iranian philosophy student. I think about the fact that the refugees I am meeting here all speak Farsi, or Arabic, or Urdu, or Dari. That the refugee crisis is predominantly made up of people of color, from Muslim communities. This perhaps is the thing that strikes me the

most. I wonder, if they were all white or all Christian, would European political leaders treat them the same way?

Time and again people tell me that the camps are hell. "It is hell, it is hell, it is hell." They tell me that the EU purposely keeps the camps unlivable, so as to act as a deterrent. "Moria is entirely consistent with European values," a volunteer from the UK tells me. "This is the continent that built the concentration camps after all, let's not kid ourselves that Moria is some aberration in its history. Europe has done terrible things before."

I shake my head to rid it of my thoughts and pour myself a strong coffee before joining the group of volunteers working through checklists with the adults for what they might need. Essential items such as shoes, soap, underwear, toothbrushes, towels, and blankets are gathered from Home for All's warehouse next door to the restaurant and, as I speak Farsi, I end up wandering around the tables with a pen and paper in hand and scribbling down requests for a shawl, diapers for children, sanitary products for women, sandals. The group I spend most of my time with are a set of Afghan families who were living in Iran and who arrived on the island just a few days earlier. One of the women is eight months pregnant and as she sits, resting swollen ankles, she calls me over and asks in a hushed voice if she can have two portions of food, one for now and one to take back with her. I wonder, not for the first time, how brave and strong and desperate a person has to be to attempt to be smuggled across borders while carrying an unborn baby.

"This place is not only about food," Katerina tells me. "We wanted to create a caring environment where people can forget about their worries for just a moment and feel human again." Ten feet away from us, a group of teenage boys have gathered around one of the tables for a guitar lesson with a Greek volunteer. Their gentle, melodic strumming echoes around the courtyard outside the restaurant.

"I believe that everyone has the right to be safe," Katerina goes on. "To be free from hunger. To be acknowledged and to feel at home, regardless of their nationality or asylum status. But our government isn't providing that," she continues, "so we have to provide."

We are eating lunch as we talk, in the main room of the restaurant, the tables around us full of chattering families. Today's menu is pot-roast lamb, tender on the bone, served with a golden rice pilaf flecked with small pieces of carrots, green beans, and peppers.

"What made you do this?" I ask. "To stop your business, your restaurant, and put all your energy into providing a free service for refugees?"

"I think the people that arrive here deserve what all of us have," Katerina says. "To sit on a chair, eat food at a table, to drink out of glass. When we first started distributing food, we took it to the camps and I remember watching a young man take what we gave him, in plastic, and walk around trying to find a place to eat it. Eventually he squatted on the edge of a small rock. Being able to eat in our place, in this comfort, at a table, with proper cutlery, it restores people's dignity, it reminds them who they are. It makes them feel they are at home. It was the refugees that came up with the name, they kept saying, 'it feels like home, it feels like home.' So we called the space Home for All."

I finish my lunch and join a table with the Afghan women I'd met earlier, relishing the opportunity to practice speaking Farsi again, which is mostly the same as the Afghan language, Dari. I strike up a conversation with Mozhdeh, a young Afghani-Iranian who is bright-eyed, smart, beautiful, and full of the hopeful optimism of youth. After I fail to get some salient points across in my broken Farsi, with laughter we realize that instead we can speak English together, in which is she completely fluent. We share memories of Tehran and the delights of Northern Iranian food, exchanging recipes for our favorite dishes. I ask her to tell me about Afghan food, of which I know little, but—just as our languages also cross regional borders—we come to find common understandings of dishes through the Pakistani food I know from my father, which has many similarities with Afghan cuisine. We both agree that *Kashk e bademjan* (see page 105)—an eggplant dip—is our favorite Iranian appetizer.

After a time, we return to larger subjects, and talk of Mozhdeh's present and her future. She wears a hijab, but nonchalantly, as more of a nod to the garment, in the style of so many Iranian women I know, with the scarf loose above her forehead and her black hair showing.

"I had to leave Iran because of my dreams," she tells me. "They won't come true in Iran, because I'm Afghan and so I am of the lowest importance for Iranian people. The way Afghans are treated in Iran is like second-class citizens; you don't have the same opportunities or the chance to work. If you are Afghan in Iran, even if you are born there, you don't have the same rights."

The United Nations states there are around three and a half million Afghans in Iran; a mixture of refugees, those with settled status, and undocumented migrants who've fled successive wars in their country over the last forty years. Many like Mozhdeh were born in Iran, but even that doesn't give equal rights.

"A country is just a name," Mozhdeh continues. "I don't believe in countries or borders. There is one earth and it's for God, for Allah. It doesn't belong to anybody. We should have the right to move and live where we feel." "Have you always felt that way?" I ask. "Yes!" She replies solidly, with an air of defiance that I can relate to. For when you grow up with several nationalities in your orbit, borders start to become meaningless.

"After this is over, I want to continue my education," she tells me. "To go back to college and expand my horizons. To set an example for Afghan women. Do you think I can do it?"

I tell her that I have no doubt she can do anything she sets her mind to.

As the evening draws to a close, the minivans reappear and the volunteers—internationals of all ages from Spain, the Netherlands, the UK, and Germany—start handing out bags filled with the goods they were able to find at the warehouse. People start to prepare for their journey back to the camps.

"What have you learned from doing this?" I ask Katerina, as we wave off a group. Katerina looks out at the sea, contemplating her answer. "I think I'm a completely different person after all of this. The act of giving has changed me. And I think it's made me a better person. Before, I always wanted things: a better car, something for the house, a new dress. Now I've learned that we have to be thankful for the basic necessities that we have, because others don't have them."

"Did this happen gradually?" I ask, as we turn back to the restaurant, about to close up its doors for another night.

Katerina shakes her head, smiling. "No, my perspective changed in a minute. Just one minute. When we got back from meeting that group of refugees on the beach that first night, it was late and I was looking forward to going home, ordering a pizza, going to sleep. But when I put my key in my front door and entered my house, everything changed. I looked at everything with new eyes. I saw a glass on my coffee table. Just a glass, and I thought, 'See what you have now? You have this glass. And this telephone. And this refrigerator. You can sit at a table and eat. And take a shower. And get into your comfortable bed. You have a house.' One hour before, I was at the beach watching strangers come into shore, and helping them get out of the boats with absolutely nothing, and I mean, nothing. I realized in that moment that I don't have to ask for more things. I have more than enough. And from that moment, the way I see life, I see things, changed completely. And slowly, it led to all of this. The way I see it is, if you can help, you just do it."

SOUPS

This book began, as so many things do in my life, with a conversation over a meal. More specifically, a conversation over a pumpkin soup, sweetened with cardamom and enriched with coconut milk. I was visiting some friends, Glynn and Stephanos, in Berlin, and, one evening, I sat watching Stephanos, a Greek Cypriot, prepare dinner. As well as the soup there were beef meatballs seasoned with spearmint and wild oregano that sizzled and sputtered as they fried in a pan; and a dish of celery root, roasted in the oven then mashed with a fork and seasoned with orange juice and Cypriot olive oil. The ingredients were familiar but the combinations surprising and, before long, I was quizzing Stephanos about the food, culture, and politics of Cyprus. By the end of dinner, after several glasses of wine, we were poring over maps and books and it was decided: I was going to Cyprus! And today, every time I make that elegant soup—which is in no way a classic Cypriot recipe but wholly a concoction of my Cypriot friend in a globalized community—I am reminded of Stephanos, who first set me off on a culinary adventure around his home country.

. . . .

Soups feature heavily in Eastern Mediterranean cuisine, especially in Turkey where they are a celebrated part of daily meals and enjoyed at all hours, from first thing in the morning, for breakfast (they are reported to be the best hangover cure) to last thing at night, on the way home from an evening's revelry (they are also reported to be the best hangover prevention). Soups in Turkey are often also associated with folklore and traditional customs and are distributed for wakes, weddings, and local festivals. So it's no surprise that, when you walk around major Turkish cities, it's common to see cafés dedicated solely to soup, with fifteen or twenty varieties on offer at almost any time of the day or night.

Turkish bride soup

EZOGELİN ÇORBASI

A soup with a story behind it. Or perhaps I should say several stories, as with all good folklore. One version is this: there was a beautiful young woman named Ezo, who lived in a village in Gaziantep near the Turkish-Syrian border. Ezo struggled greatly when it came to finding matrimonial bliss; her first marriage ended when her husband fell in love with another woman and her second marriage took her far from home, to Syria, where she became deeply homesick and struggled with her mother-in-law. It is said that Ezo created this soup to win her mother-in-law around to her favor. Today, it is fed to brides on their wedding day to sustain them for the uncertain future ahead, and it is also found in almost every *kebapçı* (kebab restaurant) in Turkey, where it is often eaten for breakfast. Don't skip the lemon juice before serving, it really enlivens the dish.

2 tablespoons salted butter
2 tablespoons vegetable oil
1 medium onion, finely chopped
1 celery stalk, very finely chopped
1 medium carrot, very finely chopped
4 garlic cloves, finely chopped
1 cup/200g red lentils, rinsed
⅓ cup/70g fine bulgur wheat, rinsed
3¼ cup/750ml chicken or vegetable stock
1½ quarts/1.5 liters just-boiled water
1 teaspoon sweet paprika
3 tablespoons tomato paste
½ teaspoon *pul biber* (Aleppo pepper), or other mild chile flakes, plus more to serve
1 teaspoon dried oregano
2 tablespoons lemon juice
1 tablespoon dried mint
3 tablespoons extra-virgin olive oil, plus more to serve
salt and black pepper

To serve
lemon wedges
Greek-style yogurt (optional)

SERVES 4

Melt the butter with the vegetable oil in a large saucepan over low heat. Add the onion and fry for 5 minutes, then add the celery and carrot and cook for another 10 minutes with the lid on, adding the garlic for the last minute or so.

Tip in the lentils, bulgur wheat, stock, and hot water, then cover and cook for 15 minutes. Now add the paprika, tomato paste, *pul biber*, oregano, ½ to 1 teaspoon salt (depending how salty your stock is), and ¼ teaspoon black pepper. Place the lid back on the pan and cook for 15 minutes, stirring every so often so the soup doesn't catch, and adding 1 cup/240ml more water if it starts to get dry.

Lastly, add the lemon juice, dried mint, and extra-virgin olive oil and cook for a final 5 minutes. Taste to adjust the seasoning: lentils almost always need a good amount of salt to give them flavor, so don't shy away from adding more.

Serve in warmed bowls with lemon wedges, a drizzle more olive oil, and a sprinkling of *pul biber*, adding a spoonful of yogurt if you wish.

Hot yogurt & spinach soup

YAYLA ÇORBASI

This rich and creamy soup is inspired by the high mountain meadows in Northern Turkey where the country's best dairy products comes from. It's incredibly simple, quick, and comforting and, as such, is on steady rotation at my house. To make sure the yogurt doesn't split while you are cooking it, add it in stages and warm it up gently. And, as always, make sure you cook this with the best-quality full-fat plain yogurt, as low-fat varieties simply won't cut it, especially not in a soup like this where the yogurt is the star.

For the soup
scant ½ cup/85g short- or medium-grain white rice (I use Turkish baldo rice, but arborio rice would also work)
1 quart/1 liter hot chicken stock
1¾ cups/500g full-fat Greek-style yogurt
1 extra-large egg yolk
1½ tablespoons cornstarch
¾ cup plus 2 tablespoons/200ml lukewarm water
1 teaspoon dried mint
7 oz/200g spinach, roughly chopped
salt and white pepper

For the topping
3 tablespoons salted butter
1½ tablespoons dried mint
1½ teaspoons *pul biber* (Aleppo pepper), or other mild chile flakes

SERVES 4

Rinse the rice under running cold water for a few minutes so the starch washes out, then place it in a large saucepan. Pour in the hot stock, cover, and simmer for 12 to 15 minutes, until the rice is cooked.

In a bowl, whisk together the yogurt, egg yolk, cornstarch, and lukewarm water until smooth.

When the rice is cooked, take a ladleful of its cooking broth and add it to the cold yogurt mixture, whisking as you do so to warm it up. Then take the saucepan with the rice in it off the heat and very slowly, half a ladle at a time, spoon in the yogurt mixture, whisking all the time so it doesn't split.

Return the soup to medium-low heat and add the mint and ½ teaspoon each of salt and white pepper. Simmer for 5 minutes until the soup has thickened.

Add the spinach and cook for another 5 minutes, then taste to adjust the seasoning to your preference. In a separate small saucepan, melt the butter for the topping with the dried mint and *pul biber*.

When you are ready to serve, ladle the soup into warmed bowls, drizzle a couple of small spoonfuls of the hot chile-mint butter over each portion and serve immediately.

Spiced carrot soup

On my first night in Istanbul, my friend Julia and I headed for dinner at a local café in the hipster Cihangir neighborhood where she lived. As is customary in so many Turkish restaurants, as soon as we sat down we were brought a complimentary mug of soup to snack on while we looked at the menu. On this occasion it was a hearty cinnamon-spiked carrot soup, which was just what I needed to ground me and welcome me to this beautiful city.

2 tablespoons olive oil
2 tablespoons salted butter
1 medium onion, finely chopped
1 medium potato, peeled and
    finely chopped
1 teaspoon ground coriander
½ teaspoon ground cinnamon
1 lb/450g carrots, peeled and
    chopped
5 cups/1.2 liters vegetable or
    chicken stock
salt and white pepper

SERVES 4

Heat the olive oil and butter in a large saucepan. Add the onion and sauté for 5 minutes over medium heat.

Add the potato, coriander, and cinnamon and stir-fry for 1 minute, then add the carrots, stock, 1 teaspoon salt, and ¼ teaspoon white pepper. Bring to a boil, then lower the heat and simmer for 20 minutes until the carrots have softened.

Blend the soup, then adjust the seasoning to your taste. Serve in warmed bowls.

Lemon chicken soup

AVGOLEMONO

This is my take on the classic Greek chicken soup packed with veggies, herbs, and lots of lemon. Tempering the eggs makes this soup feel lusciously creamy without the need for any dairy and eating it takes me back to the streets of Athens. It's a fairly straightforward recipe, but does require some care when you are tempering the eggs, so they don't curdle. Go slowly the first time you make it to avoid any errors, and after you've added the eggs try to ensure the soup doesn't come to a boil as that's what can make it split. Even if you are reheating portions, keep the saucepan over low heat and warm it gently.

1 lb 2 oz/500g skinless chicken thighs on the bone
½ small white onion (about 3½ oz/100g), finely chopped
2 fat garlic cloves, minced
1 small celery stalk, finely chopped
1 medium carrot, finely chopped
¾ teaspoon ground cinnamon
¼ teaspoon ground turmeric
2 bay leaves
3¼ cup/750ml chicken stock
2 cups/480ml just-boiled water
scant ½ cup/90g short- or medium-grain white rice, rinsed
3½ oz/100g kale, stalks removed, leaves shredded
3 extra-large eggs
1 teaspoon finely grated unwaxed lemon zest
6 tablespoons lemon juice, or to taste
1 to 2 tablespoons chopped dill, or to taste
extra-virgin olive oil
salt and black pepper

SERVES 4 TO 6

Place the chicken, onion, garlic, celery, carrot, cinnamon, turmeric, bay leaves, stock, and hot water in a large saucepan. Season with 1 teaspoon salt and ½ teaspoon black pepper. Bring to a boil, then lower the heat, cover, and simmer for 40 minutes, until the chicken is cooked.

Spoon out the bay leaves and chicken and set aside on a plate to cool. Add the rice to the soup with another 2 cups/480ml hot water. Cover and cook for 10 minutes. Meanwhile, use your hands to shred the chicken meat from the bones into very small pieces.

After the rice has cooked, add the kale and return the chicken to the pot. Simmer for 5 minutes, then take off the heat.

In a separate bowl, whisk together the eggs, lemon zest, and juice until the mixture is foamy with no streaks remaining.

Pour 2 ladles of broth from the saucepan into a cup. Then grab a whisk and slowly add this broth to the bowl of lemony eggs, a couple of tablespoons at a time, whisking constantly. Don't pour in too much hot broth too quickly, or you'll end up with scrambled eggs. Increase to a steady stream once you are halfway through, still whisking, until you've incorporated all of it. Slowly drizzle the mixture back into the saucepan, whisking the soup constantly as you do so and incorporating it slowly.

Return the pot to low heat, add the dill, and cook for 5 minutes to allow the soup to thicken. Don't let it come up to more than a gentle simmer and, if it starts to look a bit too thick, simply loosen it with a bit of hot water.

Finally, taste and adjust the seasoning, adding a bit more lemon juice, herbs, salt, or black pepper to taste. Serve in warmed bowls with a drizzle of extra-virgin olive oil.

Pumpkin & cardamom soup

An elegant soup, enriched with coconut milk and the headiness of cardamom, that soothes and comforts beyond measure. I like to eat this with toasted, buttered sourdough bread.

2 lb 2 oz/1kg pumpkin or butternut
    squash, peeled and cut
    into 1¼-inch/3cm chunks
olive oil
1 medium onion, finely chopped
1 medium carrot, finely chopped
1 celery stalk, finely chopped
1 medium potato, finely chopped
½ teaspoon cumin seeds
seeds from 5 green cardamom
    pods, crushed
1½-inch/4cm piece of ginger,
    peeled and finely grated
2 fat garlic cloves, crushed
2 cups/480ml vegetable stock
1 x 13.5-oz/400ml can of coconut
    milk (reserving 4
    tablespoons/60ml for garnish)
salt and white pepper

SERVES 4

Preheat the oven to 400°F/200°C.

Place the pumpkin or squash in a roasting dish and drizzle with 2 tablespoons olive oil and ½ teaspoon salt. Transfer to the oven and bake for about 25 minutes, until just cooked through.

Meanwhile, heat some oil in a large saucepan over medium heat. Add the onion, carrot, celery, and potato and stir well. Place a lid on the pan so the vegetables can "sweat."

Toast the cumin and cardamom seeds by placing them in a dry frying pan over medium heat for 1 minute or so until their aromas are released, then grind the spices in a mortar and pestle and add them to the onions with the ginger and garlic. Stir well and fry for a few minutes.

Add the stock, can of coconut milk—reserving 4 tablespoons/60ml—and ½ teaspoon white pepper. Cover and let simmer for 10 to 15 minutes, until the vegetables are soft.

When the roast pumpkin or squash is ready, add it to the rest of the vegetables and simmer for 5 minutes. Then take the soup off the heat and blend it in a food processor or with an immersion blender. Taste to adjust the seasoning; depending on the amount of salt in your vegetable stock, you may want to add a little more at this stage, or a touch more white pepper.

To serve, ladle into warmed bowls and swirl 1 tablespoon coconut milk into each.

TO THE CITY
ISTANBUL, TURKEY

The etymology of words is often contested, but I always loved the theory that the origin of the name "Istanbul" was *eis ten polin*, which in medieval Greek means "to the city." I like this because, to my mind, Istanbul is *the* city in the region. Nothing compares to its vibrancy and majesty, its complexities and contradictions, its dazzling beauty and its brooding allure. And from a culinary point of view, it is undoubtedly one of the greatest food cities in the world. A place where you would be hard-pressed to have a bad meal. On countless occasions I've had better food in some of the city's most humble cafeterias than in the fancy restaurants of New York or London.

I love walking the streets of the city, drinking fresh-squeezed pomegranate juice and snacking on half a dozen stuffed mussels, eaten in front of a street cart as the vendor squeezes a lemon wedge on to each shell. I love the tubs of *nohutlu pilav*, a buttery chickpea rice, served with sharp *turşu* (pickles), which leave your lips soft and lightly covered with a slick of grease. I love the iconic mackerel sandwiches, grilled on the promenades that line the Bosporus and washed down with *şalgam*, a salty fermented turnip drink. I love the bowls of *kelle paça* soup, made from slowly simmered sheep head and trotters, which creates a rich and meaty broth on which I sprinkle flakes of *pul biber* and take almost as if it were medicine if I ever feel unwell. I love the late night *pide*, small boats of bread topped with spiced ground lamb, tomatoes, and green peppers. And the rings of fresh *simit* bread, flecked with sesame, bought from vendors who circulate throughout the city. Or the *gözleme*, savory hand-rolled crêpes filled with chard and white cheese. And this, my friends, is just what I love about the street food.

The curious thing for me is that I am not Turkish and I have never lived in Istanbul, yet each time I visit it feels incredibly familiar. Its closeness to Iran means that the two countries share many social and cultural attitudes and customs, architecture and design, and of course food, the incredible food. In slightly more challenging ways, both countries have shared similar struggles between secularism and the conservative branch of political Islam.

While these tensions are still being worked out across Turkish society, in my eyes Turkey seems to have struck a balance between the two elements better than have many other countries of the region. Some speculate that this is because Turkey had no oil and so it was mostly ignored by foreign powers. Others argue it's because the country's Ottoman past made it harder to colonize. But whatever the reason, each time I've visited, it always feels to me like a positive example of what a secular Muslim country could look like. You can walk past an old, bearded man shuffling his prayer beads as he walks down the street, alongside a young girl in a tank top going to a protest. All of this is to say that even though I have no real connection to it myself, visiting Istanbul makes me feel like I have come home. And I often find myself wondering if this is what Iran could have been like, without the decades of interference from the US and the British.

I'm not the only one to have been drawn to Turkey in recent years. Over the last decade, the country has swelled with refugees from across the Middle East and Africa. At the time of writing, and for the fifth consecutive year, it hosts the largest refugee population in the world, with 3.6 million forcibly displaced people living there. By contrast, the two countries that are the next largest refugee hosts are Colombia with 1.8 million and Pakistan with 1.4 million. This is always a point worth remembering I think, given the debates raging in the richer Western countries such as the UK, which hosted around 125,000 refugees in 2018, or the USA, which settled around 22,500 refugees that same year.

Many of these new refugees have settled around Istanbul, including Samar al-Mallah and Yousef Alozon, Syrian refugees from Damascus who started a catering business in the city, delivering home-cooked Syrian food to local businesses and families. They kindly invited me into their home to show me how to make their specialty Syrian kibbeh and talk me through how their food business operates, innovatively organized through WhatsApp and primarily delivering to other immigrant communities from Syria, Iran, Yemen, Somalia, and Saudi Arabia. The common denominator is that they serve people who live far from home but want a taste of their memories.

Then there are the numerous community and civil society initiatives for the refugee community that I had the pleasure of visiting, from the AD.DAR center that runs classes, workshops, socials, and shared community meals for the Syrian and Palestinian diaspora, or the LIFE Project, which supports refugee communities to start and scale food businesses in the city.

So when I was invited to the apartment of Berrak Göçer—a publisher and

editor of Kurdish heritage who was born and raised in Istanbul but studied in New York—it didn't take long for our conversation to wing its way to this topic of belonging in a city that feels as though it is host to many identities. Perhaps not surprisingly, this took place in my favorite space in which to have such conversations: the kitchen.

Berrak had invited me into her home to show me how to cook two family favorites of hers: a classic yogurt soup and kuru köfte, tender lamb meatballs that she served with an orzo rice pilaf. As I sat in her kitchen, she talked me through her recipes by pulling out an old notepad from her college days in NYC, where she would Skype her mum and ask her how to make the Turkish recipes she was craving abroad.

"It was so hard!" Berrak exclaims, as she leans over my shoulder to look at the page I am reading, examining her neat handwriting scripting a shopping list: four tomatoes, two green peppers, a potato, rice. "My mom cooks with her eyes and doesn't know any specific measurements, so trying to get a recipe from her was difficult," Berrak says. "It took a lot of trial and error to get things right." Berrak's notepad is filled with handwritten recipes for stews, soups, meatballs, and stuffed vegetables, some of them marked with a star and with "winner" or "keeper" scribbled next to them. She flicks through the pages with a look of amusement in her eyes. "You know, even these days when I read a recipe in a book, I still have to sometimes write it out myself to understand it. I don't know, it helps it make sense to me."

Berrak pours me a glass of black tea and then begins mixing ground lamb with breadcrumbs, parsley, and onion for the meatballs she rolls with her hands. "We put lots of bread in our meatballs," she tells me. "And we have a saying in Turkish: 'the more the bread, the more the meatballs.' It's like saying that if you have plenty of something, then that will turn it into plenty more of something else." I nod and make a quick translation in my head as "the more you put in, the more you get out," but decide that, from now on, I'm going to use the Turkish meatball idiom instead. It sounds much more fun.

As we prep the food, we talk about the differences among the Middle East, Europe, and the USA, places where we have both spent extensive periods of time. "I often think that people in Europe aren't clean enough," Berrak confides, chuckling, "That's the reputation they have in Turkey. Because they don't wash fruit or vegetables, they don't wash their hands, and they wash plates in a dirty bowl and leave detergent all over it! In Turkey we find that very strange . . . but then again, the Turkish are obsessed with hygiene."

"Same in Iran," I tell her, smiling with that same sense of familiarity again.

"Not to mention people not taking off their shoes when they come into a house!" (In case you didn't know, this is the bugbear of most Asian communities who move to the West.)

"And as for the USA," Berrak continues, "it's so strange that people walk and eat at the same time. They eat on the street, they eat on the subway. I never understood it. You need to take a break from what you are doing to eat, to sit down, to be relaxed. That's what we do here."

As Berrak slowly pours hot chicken broth into a bowl of yogurt to temper it, so it doesn't split as it cooks in the soup, the conversation moves on to life as a Kurd in Istanbul.

"Growing up, whenever I'd tell people I was Kurdish, I'd always get a reaction," she says. " 'Oh you're Kurdish? Oh . . . but you're such a nice person!' or 'Oh, I have Kurdish friends too!' Even though I didn't suffer like other Kurds, especially those in the East, I still felt an otherness. Back then, you couldn't even speak Kurdish on the streets. There are still problems of course, but things have got a lot better."

"What are you first?" I ask, watching the pot of bubbling chicken stock into which we're about to add the thick yogurt. "A Kurd or a Turk? How does your Kurdish identity sit with your Turkish identity?" Berrak takes a ladle of hot stock and whisks it into the yogurt. "It doesn't sit anywhere," she replies. "I see myself as a citizen of the world. In fact, when we were younger and we would go on vacation, if people asked my dad where he was from, that's always what he would say: 'I'm a citizen of the world.' I grew up in a household where we were just humans, just people. I have both Kurdish and Turkish within me."

I nod, telling her I share that sentiment. When you are of mixed heritage, like Berrak and me, you carry all your cultural influences with you. It is simply your lived existence.

"Identity also depends on where you are geographically," Berrak continues, turning her attention to the meatballs now, carefully dropping them into her frying pan and watching as they splutter in the hot oil. "For example, I'm not a practicing Muslim and no one here in Turkey would describe me in that way, but culturally I am a Muslim. And when I'm abroad I am seen as a Muslim woman, so that is part of my identity too."

As we start setting the table for our lunch, I ask her the question that is at the forefront of my mind, but which I am unsure how to frame. "So," I begin, "what do you think about the idea of a separate Kurdish state?" Berrak sighs and ladles the creamy soup into our bowls. "I think the priority should be for everyone to have equal rights within Turkey before anything else. To be able to

access education, healthcare, in their own language. To have political representation, not to be thrown in jail just because they talk about these issues, to have basic human rights. That's my number one."

"And after that?" I ask.

"Look, I don't believe in states," Berrak says flatly, placing our bowls on the table. "Especially after seeing how our current government acts. I don't think it will solve anything. And I look at Israel and Palestine—which is the closest example of what could happen if we tried to create another ethnic state in this region—and I just don't see how it could work. How would we determine who can live there? There are different ethnic Kurdish groups, too. What will citizenship be based on? Genetic tests? And what do we say to people who live in an area you decide to turn into a new state, will they have to move? Where will they go? It's about rights. People want equal rights, safety, and political representation. We just have to learn to all live together, equally. It's not that hard."

MAINS

In my neighborhood in Northeast London there are around fifty Turkish restaurants within a one-mile radius of my house and, somehow, they are all busy almost every night of the week with hungry locals tucking into the city's most perfect kebabs.

Walk into any of them and the scene will be largely the same: Anatolian pop music comes through the speakers as the smell of searing meat drifts out from the hooded charcoal grill. Next to the grill there is always a sturdy middle-aged man, dressed all in white, his thick fingers deftly turning skewers of juicy lamb chops, their fat sizzling and sputtering onto the hot charcoal. Another chef will sit next to him, threading tomatoes and long green peppers onto metal skewers before placing them over the flames to cook until soft and charred. Before long, your table will groan with crispy zucchini fritters, thick yogurt with smoky mashed eggplant, and charred flatbreads. These, of course, are just the warm-up act before the main events of spicy ground lamb adana, saffron-hued chicken shish, or fillets of grilled mackerel. Yes, I know, kebabs aren't the only Eastern Mediterranean main meals, but sometimes I think they could be and that—given their quality and variety—no one would really mind.

• •

There is a heartiness to Eastern Mediterranean main courses; these are meals best enjoyed once the sun has gone down and the cooler evening has everything to play for. The recipes here include time-honored classics with modern touches, as well as dishes inspired by the refugee population I met. Others are my take on traditional recipes, which reflect my personal taste. Alongside these dishes, you're going to want smaller, lighter accompaniments, so it's best to mix and match your menu with dishes from the earlier chapters, adding a salad, some yogurt, pickles, or wilted greens to your table. And of course, to eat the Eastern Mediterranean way, don't plate these individually, but put everything in the middle of the table for everyone to share and help themselves to seconds (or thirds).

Black-eyed peas with chard

LOUVI

Often, the most rewarding meals of my travels don't come from expensive dinners in fancy restaurants, but from stumbling into a roadside café when I'm very hungry. This is one of those. As I stepped out into Nicosia's central bus terminal on a sweltering hot August afternoon, I spotted a small, no-frills café on the corner of the busy intersection. The café's half a dozen plastic tables were filled with Cypriots eating huge bowls of *louvi*, a popular local dish of black-eyed peas with chard, alongside crusty bread, salty olives, a few thick wedges of tomato, and rings of raw white onion. When the waitress approached me, I enthusiastically gestured for a bowl of the same. I was not disappointed. The peas were fresh, the seasoning subtle, and the chard added its bright lemony touch. As always in a dish this simple, use the best extra-virgin olive oil you can afford. It's worth every penny in flavor and it should accompany you to the dining table so guests can add extra to their taste along with some sliced tomatoes, cucumber, raw onions, lemon wedges, and olives.

1¼ cup/250g dried black-eyed peas
extra-virgin olive oil
2 tablespoons sunflower oil,
    plus more if needed
1 medium onion, finely chopped
3 fat garlic cloves, minced
1 lb 2 oz/500g chard, leaves roughly
    chopped, stalks finely chopped
1½ teaspoons cumin seeds
generous pinch of nutmeg
1 cup/240ml vegetable stock
finely grated zest of
    1 unwaxed lemon
3 tablespoons lemon juice,
    or to taste
salt and black pepper
cilantro leaves, to serve (optional)

To serve
extra-virgin olive oil
good-quality bread
thick slices of tomato,
    cucumber, and raw onion
lemon wedges
green or black olives

SERVES 4
with bread and salad
accompaniments

Rinse the peas and soak them in a bowl of cold water with 1½ tablespoons salt for 8 hours, or overnight.

Drain and rinse the peas and place them in a large saucepan. Add just-boiled water to cover the peas by 1¼ inches/3cm, then add ¼ teaspoon salt. Bring the water to a boil for 5 minutes, spooning off any scum that rises to the top. Decrease the heat to medium-low, cover, and cook for 30 to 45 minutes, or until the peas are soft. After 20 minutes, add 2 tablespoons olive oil.

Heat the sunflower oil in a large saucepan, add the onion, and fry over low heat for 15 minutes. Add the garlic and half the chard stalks (use the rest for a soup) and cook for 5 minutes.

Toast the cumin seeds by placing them in a dry frying pan over low heat until their aromas are released, then grind them in a mortar and pestle. Add the cumin to the chard stalks with a generous pinch of nutmeg. Fry for a few minutes, adding more oil if you need it, then turn off the heat.

Add the cooked peas to the pan with the stock, chard leaves, lemon zest, lemon juice, 3 tablespoons extra-virgin olive oil, 1 teaspoon salt, and ¼ teaspoon black pepper. Cook for about 5 minutes, or until the chard leaves have wilted. Taste and adjust the seasoning with salt, pepper, or lemon juice. Peas need lots of salting, so be generous! Scatter the chopped cilantro leaves on top just before serving warm, or at room temperature, with the accompaniments. I always pour oil on my serving before eating it and encourage others to do the same.

Chana masala

Growing up, this was a regular midweek dinner in our house, cooked by my Pakistani dad. So it was a delight to see it on the menu at the Nan restaurant in Lesvos (see page 137) and to hear that the recipe had originated from a refugee cook of Pakistani descent who worked there. I suggest that you gauge the cooking time for this yourself, as brands of canned chickpeas can vary widely. Some supermarket versions in the UK need a solid hour of cooking to become soft (and can take even longer if they are organic), whereas some imported brands just need thirty minutes. In the US, I find canned chickpeas are very soft when you open them, so the lesson—as ever—is to taste as you go along. You are aiming for the chickpeas to be so tender that they simply melt in your mouth. Serve this with flatbreads or white rice, a crisp chopped salad with plenty of tomatoes and cucumber, plain yogurt, and savory mango or lime pickle on the side. Delish!

3 tablespoons vegetable oil
1 medium onion, finely chopped
1 teaspoon cumin seeds
1 teaspoon coriander seeds
4 fat garlic cloves, finely chopped
1½-inch/4cm piece of ginger,
   peeled and finely chopped
1 teaspoon garam masala
¼ teaspoon ground turmeric
pinch of cayenne pepper,
   or chile flakes
2 x 15-oz/425g cans of chickpeas,
   drained and rinsed
1 medium tomato, skinned
   (see page 59) and chopped
1 tablespoon tomato paste
2 cups/480ml just-boiled water
1 teaspoon cornstarch
2 tablespoons extra-virgin olive oil
finely chopped cilantro leaves,
   to serve (optional)
salt and black pepper

SERVES 4

Heat the vegetable oil in a large pan over medium-low heat. Add the onion and fry for 15 to 20 minutes until completely soft and golden brown, stirring regularly. (This stage is crucial in creating the base flavor of this dish, so please don't rush it!)

Toast the cumin and coriander seeds in a dry frying pan over medium heat for 1 minute or so, until their aromas are released. Grind in a mortar and pestle, then add them to the onion with the garlic, ginger, and ground spices. Fry for a few minutes.

Add the chickpeas, tomato, tomato paste, hot water, 1½ teaspoons salt, and a generous grind of black pepper. Cover and cook over medium heat for 45 to 60 minutes, or until the chickpeas are completely soft and plump. Check on it halfway through cooking and add another 1 cup/240ml of hot water if the chickpeas look a bit dry.

Taste to adjust the seasoning, then stir in the cornstarch. Cook for a few final minutes for the sauce to thicken, then take off the heat and finish with the extra-virgin olive oil.

Scatter with finely chopped cilantro, if you like, and serve with warm flatbreads or white rice.

Mushroom moussaka

When I was staying in the village of Plomari, on the southern coast of Cyprus, I had the most extraordinary vegetarian moussaka one evening in a small taverna in the center of the town. It confirmed for me that vegetable moussakas are just as good as those that are lamb-based . . . and that I must include a recipe in this book. It's best to let the moussaka rest for about 20 minutes after it has come out of the oven, both so the béchamel can firm up and to make it easier to cut, so bear this in mind when you are working out what time you want to eat. I use a 2½-quart/2.5-liter oven dish that is 14 x 10 inches/35 x 25cm in shape. You want it to be deep enough for a couple of layers of eggplant. Serve with bread or orzo and some wilted kale, dressed with a squeeze of lemon juice and extra-virgin olive oil.

scant 1 oz/25g dried mixed wild mushrooms (porcini, oyster, black trumpet, and so on)
olive oil
3 to 4 large eggplants (total weight about 2⅔ lb/1.2kg) cut in rounds about 1 inch/2.5cm thick
1 medium onion, finely chopped
3 fat garlic cloves, minced
½ teaspoon ground cumin
1½ lb/700g brown button mushrooms, chopped into 1¼-inch/3cm chunks
1 teaspoon ground cinnamon
1 teaspoon sweet paprika
2 teaspoons dried oregano
1½ cups/400g uncooked tomato purée
1 teaspoon granulated sugar
1¼ cups/25g parsley leaves, chopped
1 cup/100g plain breadcrumbs (store-bought is fine)
salt and black pepper

For the sauce
2¾ cups/650ml whole milk
¼ cup/60g salted butter
½ cup/60g all-purpose flour
½ cup/60g grated *kefalotyri* or Parmesan cheese
¼ teaspoon white pepper
⅛ teaspoon freshly grated nutmeg
2 extra-large eggs, lightly beaten

SERVES 4 TO 6

Preheat the oven to 425°F/220°C. Rinse the dried mushrooms and place in a bowl. Cover with just-boiled water and set aside to rehydrate. Lightly brush a baking sheet with oil, add the eggplant in a single layer and toss with 3 tablespoons oil and ¾ teaspoon salt. Bake for 25 to 30 minutes until soft.

Heat 3 tablespoons more oil in a large saucepan over medium heat. Add the onion and sauté for 15 minutes. Add the garlic and cumin and fry for a couple of minutes. Then add the fresh mushrooms, cinnamon, paprika, and oregano. Fry for 5 minutes. Drain the dried mushrooms and add them to the pan with the tomato purée, sugar, parsley, and 1½ teaspoons salt. Cook for 5 minutes over high heat to evaporate some of the water. Add the breadcrumbs, stir well, and take off the heat.

Now for the sauce. Heat the milk until it is just below boiling point. Melt the butter in another saucepan over low heat, add the flour, and cook for 3 minutes, stirring frequently. Slowly whisk in the hot milk and keep stirring until you have a thick sauce. Once you do, add the cheese, ½ teaspoon salt, the white pepper, and nutmeg and whisk until the cheese melts.

If you are baking this straight away, take the sauce off the heat and allow it to cool for 5 minutes before beating in the eggs. If you are finishing the dish later, simply beat the eggs into the sauce just before you start assembling the moussaka.

Preheat the oven to 400°F/200°C. Arrange half the eggplants in the oven dish and spoon the mushrooms over the top. Add another layer of eggplants, covering the mushrooms completely, then pour in the sauce. Bake for 45 minutes or until well browned. Let cool for 20 minutes, then serve.

Tagliatelle with herbed lentils

HARAK OSBAO

This recipe is inspired by a visit to AD.DAR, a Syrian and Palestinian-Syrian community center in Istanbul. Among its many activities, the center places great emphasis on cooking family-style meals for the community several days each week. I wanted to include this recipe in the book after talking to Syrian refugees from the city of Aleppo, whose signature flavors include the sweet-and-sour tang of pomegranate molasses. The name of the dish translates from Arabic as "he burned his finger," which goes some way to explaining how irresistible it is, even when it's piping hot. It makes a very filling vegan main, or a lovely addition to a mezze spread.

1 cup/200g brown lentils
2 cups/480ml vegetable stock
1 teaspoon ground cumin
2 medium red onions
2 tablespoons sunflower
    or vegetable oil
3 garlic cloves, crushed
10½ oz/300g tagliatelle
3 tablespoons pomegranate
    molasses, or to taste
6 tablespoons/90ml extra-virgin
    olive oil, plus more to serve
1 tablespoon lemon juice
1 cup/20g cilanro leaves and stalks,
    finely chopped
1 cup/20g parsley leaves, finely
    chopped
¾ cup/15g mint leaves, finely
    chopped
¼ cup/35g pine nuts
2 handfuls of pomegranate seeds
salt and black pepper

SERVES 4

Rinse the lentils in cold water and place them in a saucepan. Pour in the stock and add the cumin, cover, and simmer for 20 to 25 minutes. Depending on the age and quality of the lentils, you may need to add up to another 1 cup/240ml just-boiled water halfway through cooking. You're aiming for the lentils to have absorbed all the water when they are cooked, so keep adding small amounts of hot water if you see them drying out, and cook until they are completely soft.

Meanwhile, slice the red onions into half-moons around ¼ inch/5mm wide. Heat the vegetable oil in a large frying pan over medium heat and add the onions. Fry for 20 minutes, stirring regularly, until the onions are soft, then add the garlic and fry for another couple of minutes. Take off the heat and set aside.

Bring a large pan of water to a boil. Add 1 tablespoon salt and the tagliatelle and cook according to the package instructions. Drain and set aside.

Whisk together the pomegranate molasses, extra-virgin olive oil, lemon juice, ½ teaspoon salt, and ½ teaspoon black pepper. Pour this over the tagliatelle and stir in the onions, lentils, and three-quarters of the herbs. Toss everything together well (it will start to smell amazing at this point). Taste and adjust the seasoning with a touch more salt and pepper, or a bit more pomegranate molasses if you like its sweet-and-sour tang.

Finally, toast the pine nuts in a small dry frying pan over medium heat for 1 to 2 minutes until they are golden brown.

To serve, place the tagliatelle and lentils in a large serving bowl. Sprinkle with the remaining herbs, the pine nuts, and pomegranate seeds and finish with a good drizzle of extra-virgin olive oil.

Istanbul's famous mackerel sandwiches

BALIK EKMEK

Walking along the Bosporus in Istanbul, one of the most iconic sights is that of men standing at the side of the water behind small barbecues, grilling fresh mackerel for these tasty takeaway sandwiches that are best eaten staring out at the bobbing waters. My version substitutes frying the fish for grilling, but you can still cook these over coals at a barbecue if you'd prefer. They are a great way to feed a crowd.

The salad ingredients here are just a rough approximation—I'll leave it for you to judge exactly how much of each vegetable you want in your sandwich—just don't skip the mint, or the dressing, as you need its sharpness and piquancy to cut through mackerel's intense flavor.

For the dressing
2 tablespoons extra-virgin
   olive oil, plus more to serve
2 tablespoons lemon juice
1 tablespoon pomegranate
   molasses
¼ teaspoon sumac
¼ teaspoon *pul biber*
   (Aleppo pepper)
½ garlic clove, bashed
salt and black pepper

For the sandwich
¼ small red onion, or enough
   for 2 to 3 rings per sandwich,
   or to taste
2 ciabatta rolls, each cut to the
   size of a mackerel fillet
2 mackerel fillets
olive oil
small handful of mint leaves,
   roughly chopped
½ medium carrot, grated
large handful of arugula
1 ripe, juicy tomato,
   finely sliced

SERVES 2

Put all the ingredients for the dressing in an empty jar with ¼ teaspoon each of salt and black pepper. Seal the jar, then shake vigorously and set aside for 5 minutes.

Place the red onion in a shallow bowl, pour in the dressing (removing the garlic), and let marinate. (This removes some of the onion's astringency.)

Take a plate and cover it with paper towel, ready to soak up the oil from the mackerel later.

Preheat the oven to 400°F/200°C and cut the pieces of ciabatta in half. Pop the bread in the oven for 5 minutes, so it warms up and is lightly toasted.

Spoon a couple of small spoonfuls of the dressing over the flesh side of the mackerel, then season the fish generously with salt. Heat 2 tablespoons regular olive oil in a frying pan over medium-high heat. Add the mackerel, skin side down, and fry for 3 to 4 minutes. Once the skin has begun to crisp up, flip the fillets and cook for 1 to 2 minutes on the other side, until just cooked through.

While the fish is cooking, place the mint, carrot, and arugula in the bowl with the onion and toss well.

When the mackerel is ready, transfer the fish to the plate lined with paper towel and begin assembling the sandwiches.

Drizzle the toasted bread with good-quality extra-virgin olive oil. Then layer the mackerel on to the bread, followed by the tomatoes with a pinch of salt added, then the carrot mixture, then a couple of small spoonfuls of the dressing. Pop the top layer of bread on the sandwich and eat immediately!

Sea bream with pistachio & herb smash

Sea bream is one of the most popular fish in Turkey and is native to the waters of the Aegean Sea. I like to pair it with pistachios, another famed ingredient from Eastern Turkey, in this tangy, herb-packed sauce that is easy to whiz up for a quick midweek meal. This recipe serves two, but you can easily double it up and, if you don't have access to sea bream, simply substitute another firm white fish. This goes well with a simple salad and some potatoes.

For the sauce
¼ cup/30g shelled, unsalted
    pistachios
2 handfuls of parsley leaves,
    finely chopped
1 handful of dill, finely chopped
finely grated zest of
    1 unwaxed lime
2 tablespoons lime juice
1½ tablespoons small capers,
    drained and rinsed
4 tablespoons extra-virgin
    olive oil
salt and black pepper

For the fish
4 sea bream fillets
½ teaspoon ground cumin
2 tablespoons all-purpose flour
3 tablespoons vegetable oil

SERVES 2

If you have a mortar and pestle, use it to pound the pistachios until they resemble fine breadcrumbs. Otherwise place the nuts in a freezer bag and bash them with a rolling pin. Transfer the pistachios to a small bowl and add all the remaining sauce ingredients with ¼ teaspoon salt and a good grind of black pepper. Mix well to ensure the herbs and nuts are evenly coated in the dressing, then set aside for the flavors to infuse.

Pat the sea bream dry with paper towel and season the fillets with salt and black pepper before using your hands to rub the cumin into the fish's flesh. Dust the fish with the flour, evenly coating it on both sides.

Heat the vegetable oil in a frying pan over medium heat. Make sure the oil is hot, then place the sea bream in the pan, skin side down. Fry for 4 minutes, then flip it over and cook it for 30 seconds on the other side. Transfer the fish to some paper towel to soak up the oil, then serve immediately, topped with the pistachio sauce.

Fish kebabs with skordalia

This dish finds me crossing borders and bringing together the flavors of Greece and Turkey, using a Turkish fish marinade alongside a garlicky Greek potato sauce. Swordfish are commonly used in Turkey to make fish kebabs and are (at the time of writing) a good sustainable fish choice. They have a meaty texture that lends itself very well to kebabs, but you can substitute hake, monkfish, or any other firm white fish that is available; just ask your fishmonger to remove any bones and skin. You can barbecue these, or cook them under a very hot broiler. Some fries or white rice would be good accompaniments, as well as some fresh salads.

For the skordalia
1 lb 2 oz/500g floury potatoes, cut into 1¼-inch/3cm chunks
3 garlic cloves, minced
4 tablespoons lemon juice, or to taste
7 tablespoons extra-virgin olive oil
salt

For the fish
½ teaspoon cumin seeds
2 lb/900g firm white fish fillets, such as swordfish, hake, or monkfish
1 teaspoon finely grated unwaxed lemon zest
3 tablespoons lemon juice
½ teaspoon paprika
¼ teaspoon *pul biber* (Aleppo pepper), plus ½ teaspoon
1 garlic clove, minced
5 tablespoons extra-virgin olive oil
2 tablespoons salted butter

SERVES 4

Bring a saucepan of water to a boil and add 1 teaspoon salt. Boil the potatoes for 10 minutes, or until completely soft, then drain and place in a bowl. Mash the potatoes until completely smooth. Place the minced garlic cloves in a mortar and pestle with ½ teaspoon salt and mash it into a paste. Add this to the potato with the lemon juice, then slowly beat in the oil in stages until it is fully combined. Taste and adjust the seasoning to your preference; you may want to add more salt or lemon juice.

Toast the cumin seeds in a dry frying pan over medium heat for 1 minute or so, until their aroma is released. Grind in a mortar and pestle.

Cut the fish into large equal-size chunks and place them in a large bowl. Add the lemon zest and juice, spices, garlic, olive oil, and ¾ teaspoon salt, mix well, and then let marinate for 10 minutes.

Either thread the fish pieces on skewers if you are barbecuing them, or place them on a baking sheet. Preheat the broiler to its highest setting, then cook the fish for 2 minutes on each side until the pieces are just cooked through. While the fish is cooking, melt the butter in a small saucepan and mix it with the ½ teaspoon *pul biber*.

To serve, spoon the chile butter over the fish just before you bring it to the table with the skordalia dip.

Prawn saganaki

This is one of those classic Greek flavor combinations that will transport you straight to the shores of the Mediterranean coast. Ouzo is an anise-flavored aperitif that is very popular in the Eastern Mediterranean, with variations drunk in Greece, Turkey, and Cyprus. If you don't have any, you can substitute it with rakı, arak, or pastis, or leave it out entirely and simply up the fennel seeds by ½ teaspoon so you still get the aniseed flavor. The word *saganaki* in Greek refers to dishes that are cooked and served in a small frying pan, so, like its namesake, I like to make this in a large cast-iron pan that can transfer straight from the broiler to the table. Serve this with a green salad and some good bread, or orzo.

2 tablespoons vegetable oil
1 small white onion,
    finely chopped
2 garlic cloves, crushed
1 teaspoon fennel seeds
1 x 14.5oz/400g can of diced plum
    tomatoes
1 teaspoon granulated sugar
1 teaspoon dried oregano
1 cup/240ml just-boiled water
3 tablespoons ouzo or rakı
    (optional, see recipe
    introduction)
large handful of basil leaves,
    torn, plus more to serve
14 oz/400g raw king prawns,
    peeled and deveined
⅔ cup/100g feta cheese
extra-virgin olive oil
salt and black pepper

SERVES 4

Heat the vegetable oil in a deep frying pan or sauté pan over medium heat. Add the onion and fry for about 12 minutes, until softened. Add the garlic and fennel seeds and fry for a couple of minutes.

Add the tomatoes, sugar, oregano, hot water, 1 teaspoon salt, and a generous grind of black pepper. Simmer for 25 minutes over low heat with the lid on.

Once the sauce has cooked, add the ouzo and increase the heat, bringing it to a boil for a few minutes to allow the alcohol to evaporate. Then lower the heat, stir in the torn basil leaves and simmer for 2 minutes.

Heat the broiler to its highest setting.

Add the prawns to the tomato sauce and give it a good stir to ensure they get coated in the sauce. Cook for only 2 to 3 minutes until the prawns have just changed color. Then crumble the feta over the dish, transfer to the broiler and cook for a couple of minutes under high heat until the feta has melted.

To serve, drizzle with extra-virgin olive oil, add a touch more black pepper, and scatter a few more basil leaves.

Steamed garlic & chile mussels

Mussels are a regular feature on menus around the Eastern Mediterranean, either stuffed with rice for *midye dolma*, sautéed with tomatoes and feta in a saganaki, or added to fragrant fish soups. This recipe carries my favorite flavors from the region in a rich broth that deserves to be mopped up with the best crusty bread you can get your hands on. I used to be quite intimidated by cooking mussels, but they are easy to make and always worth the effort, as they transport you to the coast, which in my mind is the best place to be. Just follow the instructions carefully and be sure to not overcrowd the pan; use a large one that isn't more than half full, as mussels need plenty of space to move around as they cook.

2 lb 2 oz/1kg mussels
4 tablespoons/60g salted butter
4 shallots, finely chopped
 (total weight about 2⅓ oz/65g)
3 garlic cloves, minced
½ teaspoon sweet paprika
1 teaspoon *pul biber*
 (Aleppo pepper)
½ cup/120ml white wine (or
 substitute 7 tablespoons/100ml
 water and 2 tablespoons lemon
 juice)
3 tablespoons finely chopped
 parsley leaves
lemon juice, to taste
salt and black pepper
crusty bread, to serve
lemon wedges, to serve

SERVES 2
as a main with bread and *Horta* (see
page 101) or a salad

Tip the mussels into the kitchen sink and give them a good rinse and scrub under cold water. Use a butter knife to scrape off any barnacles (the solid white bits attached to some shells) and pull out any beards (the wispy hair-like strands that may also be attached).

Inspect the mussels as you go, discarding any that have broken shells or that remain open. If any mussels are open, tap them sharply against the side of the sink. If they don't close, throw them away. The cleaning and prep will take a good 15 minutes (or more, depending on the mussels), and—to be honest—about halfway through I always get fed up with all the scraping, pulling, and rinsing and want to give up. But it is always worth it, so bear that in mind as you persevere.

Take a large saucepan and place it over medium heat. Melt the butter in the pan and gently fry the shallots and garlic for 3 minutes. Season with a generous grind of black pepper, ½ teaspoon salt, the paprika, and *pul biber*.

Pour in the wine and increase the heat to medium-high. Tip in the mussels, cover with a lid, and steam for about 4 minutes, shaking the pan every minute or so to ensure they cook evenly.

Remove the lid and take a peek: mussels are cooked when their shells have opened. Once done, remove the pan from the heat, add the parsley, and give everything a stir. Have a rummage around the pan and discard any mussels that have not opened, as they are inedible. Taste the sauce and adjust the seasoning with a bit of lemon juice or salt to your taste.

To serve, spoon the mussels into a shallow bowl and pour in the broth. Serve with crusty bread and lemon wedges.

Herb & paprika chicken

You can't go wrong with this golden roast chicken, marinated in Mediterranean herbs and spices and spatchcocked so it cooks more evenly, keeping it nice and juicy. A technique I've been playing with recently is using baking powder to dry out chicken skin, which helps it to crisp up. The longer you allow the baking powder and salt to do this, the better the effect, but I have found that even a brief amount of time helps. Of course, once you've let a chicken rest (which you need to do for succulence) the skin will soften anyway, but if you wanted to give it a go, I've included the hack below. I like to serve this with a mustardy salad and some orzo pasta or crusty bread on the side.

For the chicken
3½ lb/1.6kg free-range or organic chicken
¼ teaspoon baking powder
½ teaspoon salt

For the marinade
4 tablespoons olive oil
4 garlic cloves, minced
1½ teaspoons dried oregano
1¼ teaspoons sweet paprika
1½ tablespoons thyme or lemon thyme leaves
finely grated zest of 1 unwaxed lemon
1 tablespoon lemon juice
salt and black pepper

For the salad (optional)
4 large handfuls of crisp lettuce leaves
5 radishes, thinly sliced (and the radish tops, roughly torn, if you have them)
1 medium carrot, shaved using a vegetable peeler
2 tablespoons extra-virgin olive oil
2 teaspoons red wine vinegar
¼ teaspoon Dijon mustard

SERVES 4

Begin by spatchcocking the chicken. Use scissors or a sharp knife to cut down both sides of the backbone to remove it. Turn the bird over and press down firmly on its breastbone, pulling its legs out to flatten it. I also like to cut off the ends of the legs and wings by cutting along the joints.

Remove any giblets and pat the skin dry with paper towel. This bit is really important; you want the skin as dry as possible before you roast it.

Mix the baking powder and salt together and rub this over the chicken skin. Set aside for at least 20 minutes.

Now mix all the marinade ingredients together with 1 teaspoon salt and ½ teaspoon black pepper. (If you aren't doing the baking powder trick, add ½ teaspoon extra salt, to make a total of 1½ teaspoons.) Rub this on both sides of the chicken, loosening the skin under the breast bone and the thighs so you can get it right in there under the skin too. Let marinate for at least 1 hour, or up to 4 hours, covered, in the refrigerator. Return the chicken to room temperature 1 hour before you plan to begin cooking it.

Preheat the oven to 450°F/240°C and transfer the chicken to a roasting dish. When you are ready to cook, lower the oven temperature to 400°F/200°C and roast the chicken for 35 to 40 minutes, until it is browned on top and the juices run clear, basting the bird with its juices after 25 minutes. Let rest for 10 minutes, uncovered.

If you are serving the salad, assemble the lettuce, radishes, and carrot in a serving bowl. Separately whisk the oil, vinegar, and mustard together, seasoning well with salt and black pepper, and toss it with the salad. Serve with the chicken.

Veiled rice with spiced chicken

PERDE PİLAVI

This is a special occasion pilaf often served at Turkish weddings. I was taught how to cook it in the home of Melda Erdoğan, a schoolteacher in Istanbul who told me that it takes its name from the rice being hidden away under a thin "veil" of pastry, which symbolizes the building of a new home together. The pastry represents the house, the almonds and pine nuts represent the husband and wife, and the raisins are the children.

Don't be intimidated by the different stages or relatively lengthy list of ingredients, it is actually pretty straightforward to make. You'll just need to give yourself a couple of hours, and after you've made it once, you'll whiz through it next time. To break up the cooking process, you can prepare the rice filling and the dough in advance and then just assemble the dish and pop it in the oven 40 minutes before you want to eat. Or you can use leftover roasted chicken. Traditionally this is made in a copper pot, but I find it works just as well in a 9-inch/23cm cake pan or a large earthenware pot. Essential accompaniments are a lemony Turkish shepherd's salad and a big bowl of Yogurt with cucumber & mint (see pages 148 and 107), so be sure to have those on the table.

For the chicken
1 lb 3 oz/550g boneless, skinless
    chicken thighs
2 tablespoons olive oil
1 teaspoon cumin seeds,
    toasted and ground
¼ teaspoon ground cinnamon
¼ teaspoon sweet paprika
salt and black pepper

For the dough
2 tablespoons plain yogurt
2 tablespoons olive oil
1 large egg
1¼ cups/150g all-purpose flour,
    plus more to dust
½ teaspoon salt
½ teaspoon baking powder

For the rice
1½ cups/300g basmati rice
2 tablespoons salted butter
2 cups/480ml chicken stock
½ cup plus 2 tablespoons/150ml
    just-boiled water
2 teaspoons dried oregano
2 teaspoons cumin seeds,
    toasted and ground
¾ teaspoon ground cinnamon

Continued on the next page

Preheat the oven to 400°F/200°C and place the chicken on a rimmed baking sheet. Pour the oil and spices over the meat with ½ teaspoon salt and ¼ teaspoon black pepper and use your hands to rub it in evenly. Transfer the chicken to the oven and roast for about 25 minutes, until it is just cooked through. Remove from the oven and allow to cool a little, then use your hands to shred it into small pieces around ½ inch/1cm thick.

Next make the dough. Begin by whisking together the yogurt, oil, and egg in a small bowl. Place the flour, salt, and baking powder in a larger bowl and then slowly add the wet ingredients to the dry, stirring to combine. Once it is fully mixed together, use your hands to bring the dough together. It will be very sticky at first but, after you've kneaded it for a few minutes, it will form a plump ball and start looking elastic. Knead for 5 minutes, then wrap in plastic wrap and set aside while you prepare the filling.

To prepare the rice, place the grains in a sieve and rinse them until the water runs clear. Melt the butter in a saucepan over medium heat and then add the rice. Gently fry for 4 minutes, stirring occasionally so that all the grains of rice become coated in a slick of butter. Add the stock, hot water, oregano, spices, and ¾ teaspoon salt and stir well.

Continued on the next page

Veiled rice with spiced chicken *continued*

For the filling
1 small onion, finely chopped
2 tablespoons vegetable oil
¼ cup/30g sliced almonds
½ cup/70g raisins
¼ cup/30g pine nuts
2 tablespoons lemon juice
½ teaspoon *pul biber*
    (Aleppo pepper)
2 tablespoons salted butter, melted
handful of blanched almonds

SERVES 4 TO 6

Then use a few pieces of paper towel to line the top of the saucepan, stick the lid on it, and cook over low heat for 12 minutes. Check the rice: it should be mostly cooked, though still have some bite. Take the saucepan off the heat and allow the rice to rest and cool down with the lid on for 10 minutes.

While the rice is cooking, make the filling. Sauté the onion in the oil for about 10 minutes until it has softened. Add the almonds, raisins, pine nuts, lemon juice, and *pul biber* with ½ teaspoon black pepper and ¼ teaspoon salt and stir gently for a few minutes until the raisins have plumped up and the nuts begin to brown. Take off the heat and let cool.

Now you can start assembling!

Preheat the oven to 425°F/220°C. Mix the shredded chicken, filling, and rice together, using your hands to make sure all the ingredients are evenly distributed throughout the rice. At this stage, taste the rice and check if it is seasoned enough. As varieties of stock can vary, you may want more salt and pepper.

Dust a work surface with a little flour and use a rolling pin to roll out the dough very thinly so that it is large enough to cover the bottom of a 9-inch/23cm cake pan or baking dish and also wrap around the rice. It will probably need to be around 1/16 inch/2mm thick.

Generously brush melted butter on the bottom and sides of the pan or baking dish you are using. Place a few blanched almonds in the pan or dish in a circular design and gently place the dough into it, getting it to firmly line the sides of the pan.

Spoon the rice into the dough and flatten it down so it's evenly distributed in the pan or dish. Then fold the dough over on itself to completely cover the rice. Trim away any excess, as if the layers of dough overlap too much they won't cook evenly. Use a bit more melted butter to brush over the surface of the pastry and help to seal the joins.

Cover with a sheet of foil and transfer to the oven. Bake for 20 minutes covered, then another 20 minutes uncovered, until the pastry is golden. Then remove from the oven and allow to rest for 5 minutes before turning it out onto a serving plate, with the pattern of blanched almonds on top.

Pomegranate & sumac chicken

This is an easy chicken sheet pan recipe inspired by a meal I ate at Reem, a restaurant on the Greek island of Lesvos run by Mahmud Talli. Mahmud is a powerhouse of energy and, when I met him, he was splitting his time between volunteering at a local community center (One Happy Family, see page 11) and running this restaurant. A Syrian doctor who managed to escape the war, Mahmud found himself trapped on the island after seeking refuge there, and soon put all his efforts into helping to provide services for new arrivals to Lesvos. Reem serves traditional Syrian food to hungry tourists, volunteers, locals, and refugees alike and this was one of my favorite dishes on the menu, a sticky roasted leg of chicken that can be marinated ahead of time and just popped into the oven shortly before eating. If you don't want to use chicken thighs, this also works with a whole chicken, jointed into eight pieces.

For the chicken
8 large skin-on, bone-in
   chicken thighs
3 tablespoons olive oil

For the marinade
3 tablespoons pomegranate
   molasses
1 tablespoon tomato paste
½ teaspoon ground allspice
2 teaspoons *pul biber*
   (Aleppo pepper)
1 teaspoon sumac
¼ teaspoon ground cumin
2 fat garlic cloves, crushed
salt and black pepper

SERVES 4

Place the chicken in a large bowl and pour all the marinade ingredients over it with 1½ teaspoons salt and ½ teaspoon black pepper. Using your hands, massage this into the chicken until it is evenly coated, then cover and transfer to the refrigerator to marinate for at least 3 hours.

When you are ready to eat, take the chicken out of the refrigerator and let it come to room temperature (this will take about 20 minutes).

Preheat the oven to 400°F/200°C.

Place the chicken on a rimmed baking sheet and drizzle with the olive oil. Transfer the sheet to the oven and roast for about 35 minutes, or until the juices from the chicken run clear when it is pierced at the thickest part.

Rakhine chicken curry

The kitchen of the One Happy Family (OHF, see page 11) refugee community center in Lesvos was run by Mohammad, a refugee from Myanmar, who had lived and worked as a cook in India and Iran during his long passage to the Greek islands. Usually the meals made at OHF were based around vegetables but, around once a week, the kitchen would get hold of some chicken, and the cooks would make a huge vat of curry to give out for free to hundreds of refugees who visited the center each day. Mohammad, like so many others in the camps, was always very happy when it was chicken curry day at OHF. During the time I spent in the kitchen with Mohammad, he often ignored my questions if they veered into any topics too political, preferring instead to browse his playlist of songs to which he'd bop around the kitchen while cooking. So I chose not to ask him directly if he was from the Rohingya tribe, famously persecuted by the Myanmar government, but—given the circumstances of his story—assumed that to be the case. I wanted to include a recipe in this book that paid tribute to him and his bright smile, so I chose this spicy chicken curry, inspired by the food of the Rakhine state in Myanmar where the Rohingya live, and adapted from Naomi Duguid's recipe from her excellent book, *Burma: Rivers of Flavor*. The unique flavoring comes from a pungent shrimp paste and galangal, which you can find in Asian markets. If you can't access these, substitute fish sauce and ginger. Serve with white rice or nan bread.

1¾ lb/800g boneless, skinless chicken thighs
1 teaspoon ground turmeric
1½ teaspoons garam masala
1½ teaspoons ground coriander
½ teaspoon cayenne pepper, or to taste
3 tablespoons toasted sesame oil
4 shallots, finely sliced (about 7 oz/200g)
3 garlic cloves, minced
2-inch/5cm piece of galangal or ginger, peeled and finely grated
1 small hot red chile, finely chopped
2 tablespoons fish sauce or shrimp paste
1 x 14.5-oz/400g can of diced plum tomatoes
1 teaspoon granulated sugar
½ x 8-oz/225g can of bamboo shoots, drained
1¼ cups/25g cilantro leaves and stalks, finely chopped
salt and black pepper

SERVES 4

Finely chop the chicken into very small pieces, around ½ inch/1cm. Use a very sharp knife for this and be careful with your fingers, as the chicken pieces can slide around. Place in a bowl and add the ground spices and ¾ teaspoon salt. Mix well and let marinate while you make the base of the curry.

Heat the sesame oil in a large saucepan over medium heat. Add the shallots and sauté for about 10 minutes until they have softened. Then add the garlic and galangal or ginger and chile and fry for another couple of minutes. Add the fish sauce or shrimp paste, tomatoes, and sugar. Stir well, cover, and simmer for 8 minutes.

Add the chicken and bamboo shoots and cook for 10 minutes, stirring occasionally, until the chicken is just cooked through. After 8 minutes, add most of the chopped cilantro. Taste and adjust the seasoning. You may want to add a touch more salt, pepper, or cayenne.

I like to let this rest for 1 hour or so before serving, for the flavors to meld together, but you can serve it straight away too, with white rice and / or warm nan bread and the remainder of the chopped cilantro sprinkled on top.

Lamb shank kleftiko

Kleftiko is a traditional Greek and Cypriot dish, often served as the family Sunday lunch. I've heard several interpretations of where the name for the dish comes from and I like this story best: apparently, at the time of the Greek revolution of the 1820s, Greek guerrillas known as Klephts hid in the mountains, roaming as anti-Ottoman insurgents. In order to survive, they would steal a lamb or a goat as it grazed on a hillside, then cook it over many hours in a hole in the ground, sealing the hole with soil so no steam could escape to give them away. Thus came the name *kleftiko*, which refers to the stolen lamb. My version is updated, substituting my oven for a hole in the ground, and I "hide" the lamb in parcels of foil while baking it with herbs, garlic, and vegetables. Serve with a simple green salad dressed with vinegar and olive oil, or a large bowl of *Horta* (see page 101).

14 garlic cloves, unpeeled
5 tablespoons/75g salted butter, softened
olive oil
1½ tablespoons chopped rosemary needles, plus 4 sprigs
1½ tablespoons chopped thyme leaves, plus 4 sprigs
1 teaspoon dried oregano
1 teaspoon ground cumin
4 lamb shanks
1 medium onion, chopped
2 large carrots, sliced into discs
1 cup/240ml dry white wine
2 lb 2 oz/1kg floury potatoes (such as russet)
salt and black pepper

SERVES 4

Preheat the oven to 350°F/180°C.

Peel 2 of the garlic cloves and place them in a mortar and pestle. Bash them with 1½ teaspoons salt until you have a thick paste. Add this to the softened butter with 1 tablespoon olive oil, the chopped herbs, dried oregano, cumin, and a generous grind of black pepper.

Next, take a lamb shank and, using a small, sharp knife, cut 4 holes into the meat big enough to poke your finger into. Do this to all the shanks and divide the flavored butter among them, pushing it deep into the pockets and rubbing the remainder all over the meat. (At this point, you can let the meat marinate for a few hours, or overnight in the refrigerator, if you'd prefer.)

Tear off a piece of foil that is more than double the size of a lamb shank. Fold it in half, then use it to make a case for the shank, placing one-quarter of the onion and carrots and 3 whole garlic cloves in each, with a rosemary and thyme sprig. Add the lamb, season generously with salt and black pepper, then pull the sides up to create a parcel around the lamb. Just before you close the parcel, add a swig of wine, then wrap the foil tightly around it and place it on a baking sheet so that the base of the parcel with all the vegetables is at the bottom. Repeat for the remaining lamb shanks, then transfer to the oven. Roast for around 2½ hours, or until the meat is completely tender.

Continued on the next page

Lamb shank kleftiko
continued

After the lamb has been in the oven for 1¼ hours, peel the potatoes and cut them into quarters. Bring a large saucepan of water to a boil and add 2 teaspoons salt. Parboil the potatoes for 10 minutes, then drain them and return them to the saucepan. Place the lid on the saucepan and shake it so that the edges of the potatoes break up (this will make them crisp up later). Then put 5 tablespoons/75ml olive oil in a baking dish, add the potatoes, and toss them in the oil. Transfer to the oven.

When the lamb shanks are ready, take them out of the oven and let them rest for 10 minutes. If your potatoes need a bit more time, turn the oven temperature up to maximum, so they turn golden brown.

To serve, divide the potatoes between warmed plates or shallow pasta bowls, then open the lamb parcels so their lovely juices run all over the potatoes.

Adana kebabs

It's hard to pick a favorite Turkish kebab, but if I had to, this would be it, richly spiced with cumin, sumac, and cinnamon and given some heat from *pul biber* chile flakes. Essential Hackney accompaniments are flatbreads and orzo rice (double carbs are encouraged), Yogurt with cucumber & mint (or plain yogurt), Turkish shepherd's salad, and a Grilled onion salad with pomegranate & sumac (see pages 107, 148, and 160). The best way to cook these is outside over hot coals, but you can also make them inside under a broiler, or using a griddle pan. If it's the latter, turn the vent on high and open all the windows in the kitchen, as it will get very smoky.

1½ lb/700g ground lamb
  (20 per cent fat content)
1 small white onion, grated
handful of parsley leaves and
  stalks, finely chopped
3 fat garlic cloves, finely chopped
  or grated
2 teaspoons ground cumin
1½ teaspoons *pul biber*
  (Aleppo pepper)
1 teaspoon *biber salçası* (Turkish
  hot pepper paste, optional)
1½ teaspoons sumac
⅛ teaspoon ground cinnamon
salt and black pepper

To serve
a couple of tomatoes, quartered
white rice, Orzo rice (see page 79),
  and / or flatbreads such as nan
  or *taboon*
full-fat plain yogurt,
  or Yogurt with cucumber
  & mint (see page 107)
pickles and salads

MAKES 8 / SERVES 4

Combine all the ingredients for the kebabs in a large bowl with 1½ teaspoons salt and ½ teaspoon black pepper. Use your hands to pound the meat together for 5 minutes or so, really working the ingredients by squeezing them in your hands so the meat is broken down. This makes a big difference to the final texture of the kebabs, so don't skip it.

Divide the meat into 8 equal parts and mold them into long kebab shapes, around 8 skewers if you have them. Cover and refrigerate for a couple of hours, for the flavors to infuse. Take the kebabs out of the refrigerator 20 minutes before you want to grill them.

If you are cooking outside, fire up your barbecue and wait until the flames die down and the coals are white hot. Thread the tomatoes onto skewers and cook them over the hot coals until they are just cooked through (they won't need oil). Then add the kebabs, turning them every few minutes until they are browned and slightly charred. This should take 6 to 8 minutes.

If you are cooking inside, follow a similar process but under a medium-high broiler, or using a griddle pan. Start with the tomatoes, cooking for a few minutes on each side until they are cooked through. Then cook the kebabs, turning every few minutes for 6 to 8 minutes.

When the kebabs are ready, let them rest for a few minutes while you warm up the flatbreads, if using, on the same surface the kebabs were cooked on. This infuses the bread with the meat juices, making it incredibly appetizing.

Serve immediately with the all the accompaniments (and see recipe introduction).

For recipe photo, see next page

Classic Turkish meatballs

KURU KÖFTE

Wherever you are in Turkey, you won't have to look far to find cafés that specialize in different types of meatballs, and there are dozens of regional specialties that vary from town to town. This is perhaps the most stripped down and simple *köfte*, the kind your mum might make when you get home from school. It's best served with Orzo rice, Yogurt with cucumber & mint, a sharply dressed Turkish shepherd's salad (see pages 79, 107, and 148), and your favorite mild red chile sauce on the side. Just be sure to pound the meat together to get the right consistency; this will take at least a few minutes by hand. Put some elbow grease into it and you won't be disappointed.

1¾ lb/800g ground beef
1¾ cups/200g breadcrumbs
1¼ cups/25g parsley, finely
   chopped
3 garlic cloves, crushed
1 medium onion, grated
3 tablespoons water
1 extra-large egg, lightly beaten
2 teaspoons cumin seeds,
   toasted and crushed
1½ teaspoons sweet paprika
1½ teaspoons dried oregano
½ teaspoon *pul biber* (Aleppo
   pepper), or other chile flakes
¼ teaspoon baking powder
salt and black pepper
vegetable oil, to fry

MAKES 24 / SERVES 4 TO 6

Place all the meatball ingredients in a large bowl, except the oil, seasoning with 2 teaspoons salt and ½ teaspoon black pepper. Use your hands to pound everything together for a few minutes until it is completely combined and the meat has softened and looks almost paste-like. Cover and set aside in the refrigerator for at least 4 hours, or overnight, for the flavors to come together.

When you are ready to cook, take the meat out of the refrigerator and mold it into golf ball–size shapes.

Preheat the oven to 425°F/220°C. Take a large plate and line it with paper towel.

Place the largest frying pan you have over medium-high heat and add 1 tablespoon vegetable oil.

Cook the meatballs, in batches, for around 3 minutes on each side, until they are nicely browned. When you first place them in your pan, use the back of a spatula to press the balls down a little, so they form small oval patties. When they are nicely browned on both sides, transfer them to the paper towel-lined plate and cook the next batch. You may need to use a little more oil as you are frying if your pan starts to get dry.

When you've fried all the meatballs, transfer them to a rimmed baking sheet and place in the hot oven for 10 minutes until they are just cooked through.

Serve immediately with rice, breads, cucumber yogurt, pickles, and a sharp crunchy salad.

Beef stifado

This hearty Greek stew is perfect when the days start turning a little colder and has the added bonus of filling your whole kitchen with its heady, sweet scent of warming spices. As with all slow-cooked stews, it's important to use the right cut of meat, and for this I highly recommend getting down to your local butcher and buying some beef shin (off the bone). It's a very economical cut of meat and produces the best texture, proper melt-in-your-mouth stuff, not like those tough supermarket cuts of "stewing beef" from which I've never been able to produce a decent meal. Serve with orzo (the Greek/Turkish rice-shaped pasta) or mashed sweet potato, and a side of *Horta* (see page 101).

2 tablespoons all-purpose flour
¼ teaspoon ground allspice
pinch of nutmeg
2 lb/900g boneless beef shin,
    cut into 1¼-inch/3cm cubes
vegetable oil
1 medium onion, chopped
12¼ oz/350g baby shallots,
    peeled but left whole
4 garlic cloves, crushed
¾ cup/180ml red wine
1 x 14.5-oz/400g can of diced plum
    tomatoes
1 teaspoon dried rosemary
1 teaspoon dried oregano
¼ teaspoon ground allspice
¼ teaspoon ground cinnamon
2 cloves, or a pinch of
    ground cloves
1 teaspoon granulated sugar, or to
    taste
¾ cup plus 2 tablespoons/200ml
    just-boiled water
salt and black pepper

SERVES 4 TO 6

Preheat the oven to 275°F/140°C.

Mix the flour and the spices in a large bowl with ¼ teaspoon black pepper. Toss the beef pieces in it.

Heat 2 tablespoons oil in a large ovenproof casserole dish with a lid over medium-high heat. Sear and brown the beef in batches, being careful not to overcrowd them in the pan. This will take a few minutes, so no need to rush it, and if you need to add a bit more oil halfway through the cooking then go for it. Once the beef is seared, set it aside on a plate.

Lower the heat under the casserole and add a bit more oil to the pan, scraping the bottom of the pot with a wooden spoon to loosen any remnants of beef. Add the onion and shallots and cook for about 10 minutes until they've softened, then add the garlic and cook for 1 minute. Pour in the wine and scrape the bottom of the pan again to release any charred bits.

Add the rest of ingredients with 2 teaspoons salt and return the beef to the pan. Scrape the bottom of the pan again (you really want to make sure all the goodness from the bottom has dispersed through the dish), cover the cassserole, and place in the oven for 3 hours.

After 2½ hours, check on the beef and taste for seasoning. You might want to add a touch more black pepper or sugar at this stage. Cook for a final 30 minutes, or until the meat is very tender.

Greek tomato meatballs

SOUTZOUKAKIA

In Greece, these spiced meatballs are said to have originated from the Greeks of ancient Smyrna, the city now known as Izmir, on the Anatolian coast of Turkey. There are reportedly almost two hundred and fifty types of meatball recipe in Turkey, so it's not surprising that Greeks who were living in that region took on some of its most famous culinary influences. Whatever the origins, these are comfort food of the highest order. You can serve them as part of a mezze, with warm flatbreads, or for a more substantial main course, with steamed orzo or mashed potatoes and a green salad.

For the tomato sauce
2 tablespoons olive oil
1 small onion, finely chopped
2 garlic cloves, finely chopped
1 x 14.5-oz/400g can of diced plum
  tomatoes
2 tablespoons tomato paste
½ cup plus 2 tablespoons/150ml
  just-boiled water
½ teaspoon dried thyme
pinch of ground cinnamon
½ teaspoon ground cumin
½ teaspoon sweet paprika
1 bay leaf
1 teaspoon granulated sugar
salt and black pepper

For the meatballs
10½ oz/300g ground lamb or pork
10½ oz/300g ground beef
⅔ cup/70g breadcrumbs
large handful of parsley leaves,
  finely chopped, plus more
  to serve
2 garlic cloves, finely chopped
½ medium onion, grated
1 extra-large egg, lightly beaten
¾ teaspoon ground cumin
¼ teaspoon ground cinnamon
½ teaspoon sweet paprika
light olive oil, for the baking sheet
  and the meatballs
extra-virgin olive oil, to serve

SERVES 4

Begin by preparing the tomato sauce. Heat the olive oil in a medium saucepan, add the onion, and gently fry over medium heat for about 10 minutes, or until soft. Add the garlic and fry for a few minutes. Add the rest of the ingredients with ½ teaspoon salt and ½ teaspoon black pepper, stir well, cover, and let simmer for 20 minutes.

Place all the ingredients for the meatballs (except the oils) in a large bowl, season with 1½ teaspoons salt and ½ teaspoon black pepper, and mix together with your hands. Lightly oil a rimmed baking sheet, roll the meat into about 20 balls, and transfer to the sheet.

Preheat the oven to 400°F/200°C. Brush the meatballs with a little more light olive oil, then pop them in the oven and cook for 10 to 12 minutes, turning once until browned.

Add the meatballs to the tomato sauce and simmer for 15 minutes so the meat absorbs the flavors of the sauce.

Just before serving, sprinkle with chopped parsley and drizzle with extra-virgin olive oil.

THE GYPSY CHEF
ISTANBUL, TURKEY

Istanbul, famously, is a city divided by the Bosporus strait, a narrow stretch of water separating two continents: Europe on one side, Asia on the other.

It's a divide that—it has to be said—is somewhat exaggerated by visitors to Turkey who, over the centuries, have often romanticized the idea of some kind of mythical, magical difference between the two sides, a view which isn't actually reflected in the reality on the ground. And yet . . . Despite knowing all of this, and being reminded of it frequently by friends in Istanbul, there is something particularly special about the twenty-minute ferry journey, crossing this invisible continental border.

As the inky blue waves lap against the sides of the passenger boat that takes you from Karaköy (Europe) to Kadıköy (Asia Minor), it's near-impossible not to look out at the expansive skyline of palaces, minarets, high-rise office buildings, and hotels and not think for just a moment that you are a seafarer, a traveler, a true adventurer. Traversing continents somehow feels epic, even if you know it's meaningless.

I always get swept away by that crossing. Often I will amuse myself with the thought that when I make that exact same journey by metro, it takes only a few minutes, is just one stop and doesn't feel different at all. I haven't quite worked it out yet, but I put the difference down to the fact there is something intrinsically special about traveling on a boat between two shores. It's a feat that evokes a sense of accomplishment in all of us.

I travel back and forth across the Bosporus innumerable times during my weeks in Istanbul as I pop in and out of the city's kitchens, feasting on Turkish breakfasts that leave you stuffed until dinner, eating beef *köfte* and *piyaz* bean salads with activists who were prominent in the Gezi protests, and cooking with friends such as Melda Erdoğan, a history teacher of Alevi background, who teaches me about the ancient traditions of this prominent religious minority.

It is a particularly blustery April afternoon when I last make the journey across the choppy waters to visit one of my favorite restaurants in the city, the world-renowned Çiya Sofrası. As I chew on spoonfuls of pomegranate seeds I've bought from a street vendor just before boarding the boat, I scribble down questions to ask the restaurant's owner and head chef, the inimitable Musa Dağdeviren, who has made a name for himself nationally and globally as a culinary ethnographer, having dedicated his life to researching, documenting, and preserving the traditional foodways of Turkey.

Like many tourists, I visit Çiya every time I'm in Istanbul; its fast-casual, home-cooking approach to good food is much more to my taste than that of fancy restaurants with white tablecloths. Growing up with family who were farmers in Northern Iran, the methodology of Musa's approach to cuisine has always appealed to me: I share his fascination with local home-cooked foods, foraged plants, and traditional cooking techniques.

A visit to Çiya reminds me of conversations with my grandmother and always feels like a culinary education. Its unusual salads filled with twig-like greens, bitter herbs, roots, shoots, and sprigs of wild herbs are all seasonal and are sourced from far-flung corners of Turkey.

I arrive just after the lunchtime rush and head straight to the mezze bar, loading my plate with cigarillos of grape leaf dolma, pomegranate and bulgur-laced kısır, wild thyme salad, and small peppers stuffed with a dense tomato rice. The hot dish counter takes my attention next, with its myriad stews, soups, and pilafs. I order what looks like a wild asparagus and yogurt soup, a dish of braised okra with small flecks of lamb, and lastly (having recently learned how to make this at Melda's house) a miniature *Perde pilavı* (see page 227). After taking my heaving plate to the cash register—where diners pay for mezze by weight—I sit at a small wooden table at the back of the restaurant and wait for Musa to finish his lunchtime tasks, slowly eating my way through the assorted flavors, making mental notes of unfamiliar ingredients to ask him about.

Soon Musa walks over to join me, carrying the calm, unhurried air of a man who has given a thousand press interviews and knows journalists always ask the same questions. He's an intrinsically warm character, with a broad smile, plump face, and youthful eyes that twinkle. We embark on a game I imagine he plays with customers every day as he starts quizzing me about ingredients on the table. It turns out that what I thought was wild asparagus in the soup was actually the stems of foxtail lily. One of the salads I was eating included borage and milk thistle. My gasps of surprise and enchantment amuse him, and you can tell that he takes a lot of pleasure in sharing these unusual ingredients with his customers and the wider world.

As I start running through my questions, asking what set him on this

journey of food ethnography, he is at pains to stress that his restaurant and research aim to record and honor the food of the land, but without any firm attributes to ethnic ownership. "Food has no ethnicity, only geography," is Musa's mantra, one he repeats early and often. In a country such as Turkey, where national identity is heavily politicized, as it is in so many places in the world, it's a bold statement.

"I'm trying to bring forward the collective consciousness of geography," he tells me, as I tear a shard of warm buttered flatbread to wipe the dregs of the foxtail lily soup from my bowl. "I see geography as being like a mother who nurses a child, giving it knowledge that it can then bring to others. Geography is our teacher and, when we move, we take the culture or culinary knowledge that our geography has given us from one place to another."

It's an interesting use of language, I tell him, to use the concept of geography, rather than of country, as a way of delineating boundaries. Turkey, like most countries in the world, is made up of many different ethnic, religious, and cultural groups. The population ranges from Kurds, Armenians, Laz, Anatolian Greeks, Circassians, and Cretan Turks, to the more recent arrivals of Syrian, Palestinian, and Iraqi refugees.

"As soon as we label culture with religious or ethnic terms we get into disputes," Musa continues. "But these labels that we have created are the very thing that is causing conflict and dividing us." He pauses to take a sip of tea and, with a resigned tone, puts it simply. "It's borders that are the problem."

Musa was born in the city of Nizip, in Gaziantep, Eastern Turkey, close to the Syrian border. It's a region of Turkey known for its sizable Kurdish population and his father, who, like many in the region, grew olives and pistachios, was an ethnic Kurd. Musa however doesn't identify as Kurdish, a point that was raised with me before I set off on my trip to Istanbul. When I told a Kurdish friend from London that I was going to be interviewing him, she indignantly declared: "He speaks with a Kurdish accent, but he is too afraid to call himself a Kurd!" She was furious at his perceived oppression, the concealment of what she felt was his identity.

Musa laughs when I recall this story and I can tell right away this point has come up before. "I have both Kurdish and Turkish members of my family, but for me, all these labels, they just divide us, they break us up, they make monsters of each other. I'm not interested in these labels." We pause as a waiter comes to clear our table of empty plates and bring over our desserts, a large platter of candied vegetables: crunchy pieces of pumpkin topped with tahini and walnuts, halved baby eggplants sprinkled with cinnamon, and

jet-black preserved walnuts, sweetened in their shell and served with a hefty dollop of *kaymak* on the side.

As we help ourselves to the small pieces of preserved sweets, Musa warms to his theme. "I see myself as a gypsy," he says. "Sometimes I'm a Buddhist, sometimes I'm an Alevite [a sect of Islam similar to Shiism, with followers who are adherents of the mystical teachings of Imam Ali]. Sometimes I'm Sunni, sometimes Turkish; I am all of these things and none. I'm a cluster of all of these elements.

"Turkey today is a great melting pot of different cultures," he continues. "It's a wonderful big treasure box and I don't want to lock myself in as if I am a particular thing. It doesn't matter if it is a Kurd or Turk, I'm against this attitude of putting one ethnic group against another. And so I tell people I'm a gypsy, so no one can classify me in any of these ethnic groups," he says, laughing.

I like the idea of this gypsy chef, roaming freely around the country and uniting Turks of all backgrounds with his dedication to preserving the fruits of this land. But I'm curious as to how that plays out here, where the Turkish government—like governments everywhere—seems to place a strong emphasis on building a national narrative of one dominant group.

"Those in power have always wanted to keep humans in competition with each other like this," Musa tells me. "They want to pit communities against each other, to make it easier to exploit our labor and our natural resources. This is how capitalism works." He's more animated now, sitting up straighter, hands gesticulating and the tips of his fingers coming together to emphasise a point. "Capitalism would rather kill and have profit than share and keep life. It's created this pressure of competition, of having more and more and more at the expense of humanity. That's why it builds fences, to show that 'I can have more than you.' But I don't want fences, I want to learn from you and I want to teach you something. I want us to share, to exchange."

"So it's capitalism, then," I ask, "that's the real problem?"

Musa leans back into his chair and breaks into one of his broad grins, "Of course! I don't think we can get rid of borders until we overthrow capitalism."

I burst out laughing at his unbridled clarity. "I'll drink to that!" And we clink our tea glasses together.

DESSERTS

Walking around the streets of Athens, I am reminded of the many sweet delicacies of the region, from *loukamades*, tiny doughnuts filled with sugary syrup that you pop whole into your mouth, to *moustalevria*, a firm, set pudding made from concentrated fermented grape juice that carries a musky scent along with its subtle sweetness.

Or baklava, of course, the Greek version drenched in local honey with a crisp pastry that shatters when you take a bite. But my favorite sweet treat is undoubtedly bougatsa, a vanilla and semolina custard enveloped in a flaky pastry, which is then cut into squares and smothered in a cloud of confectioners' sugar and cinnamon. One of my fondest food memories of my time in Athens is sitting on a rickety table outside the Stani café, one of the city's oldest and most retro dairy bars, eating squares of this pastry as locals sat around me enjoying rice pudding, walnut pies, and thick strained yogurt topped with honey, all washed down with strong black coffee.

The desserts in this chapter celebrate the seasonal produce of the Eastern Mediterranean, from delicate sour cherries to luscious sweet figs. Traditional meals in this region end with something light and fruit based, perhaps some slices of watermelon or a spoon sweet (a type of preserved candied fruit), and it's common for restaurants to provide complimentary pieces of these, or a thin slice of semolina halva, for you to enjoy as you contemplate your bill. Of course, there are no hard-and-fast rules about when we should enjoy sweets and cakes, and—if I'm honest—many of the recipes here could be (and in my house often are) eaten for breakfast as well as for an afternoon treat.

Citrus cake

Cyprus is known for its abundance of citrus fruit and throughout the island you can find oranges, lemons, limes, pomelos, grapefruits, tangerines, and many other local varieties that blossom in its fertile Mediterranean climate. You can use any kind of citrus for this cake, though I've suggested starting with oranges and lemons. The recipe is inspired by a tangy orange cake I ate at the Home café in Nicosia, a unique space that sits within the Green Line separating the North and the South of the island. I loved the flavor so much that I immediately went to the counter and asked what was in it, and they let me in on the secret of plain yogurt in the batter, which gives the cake a lovely soft crumb. As there is a lot of zest used in this recipe, I recommend buying organic or unwaxed citrus fruit. This cake keeps well in an airtight container for a couple of days, though I doubt it will last that long.

For the cake
1 cup/225g softened unsalted
    butter, plus more for the pans
1¾ cups/225g all-purpose flour
1 cup/200g granulated sugar
4 extra-large eggs, lightly beaten
3 teaspoons baking powder
¾ teaspoon salt
1 teaspoon vanilla extract
¼ cup/55g full-fat plain yogurt
2 tablespoons finely grated
    unwaxed orange zest
2 tablespoons orange juice

For the frosting
⅔ cup/80g confectioners' sugar
12¼ oz/350g full-fat cream cheese
¼ cup/55g full-fat plain yogurt
1 tablespoon orange juice
2 tablespoons lemon juice
finely grated orange and unwaxed
    lemon zest, to serve

SERVES 8

Preheat the oven to 350°F/180°C. Butter 2 x 8-inch/20cm round cake pans and line the bottoms with parchment paper.

Place all the ingredients for the cake together in a large bowl and beat for a couple of minutes until just blended.

Divide the batter evenly between the 2 prepared pans. Bake for 20 to 25 minutes or until lightly golden. Let the cakes cool in the pans for 5 minutes, then transfer them to a wire rack.

To make the frosting, mix together the confectioners' sugar, cream cheese, yogurt, and orange and lemon juices and beat until smooth. Place this in the refrigerator to chill and firm up while the cake cools.

When the cake is completely cool, use an offset spatula to spread half the frosting on one cake. Place the other on top and cover with the rest of the frosting. Finish by decorating with a scattering of orange and lemon zests.

Pear, apricot, & rose water pudding

CHARLOTTA

This fresh and light pudding is my adaption of a traditional Cypriot dessert called *charlotta*, the basis of which is a thick and creamy rose water-scented custard. *Charlotta* epitomizes comfort and simplicity and is a favorite with Cypriot grandmas. It's traditionally made with preserved and candied fruit, but I find that a little too sweet for my taste, so have used fresh pears and dried apricots poached in a cardamom syrup. The number of ladyfingers you need depends on the shape of the serving dish, so use just enough to create an even layer. This is a straightforward recipe, but it does take a few hours to make, so read through to the end before you start so you can work out timings. You can also make it gluten-free by skipping the ladyfinger layer, as the fruit and custard are delicious on their own.

For the poached fruit and ladyfingers

2 cups/480ml water

6 tablespoons/80g granulated sugar

seeds from 7 green cardamom pods, crushed

2 tablespoons lemon juice

1 lb 6 oz/625g pears, peeled and cored, cut into 1¼-inch/3cm wedges

⅔ cup/80g dried apricots, cut into strips

about 5¼ oz/150g pre-made ladyfingers, or enough to cover the serving bowl

handful of shelled, unsalted pistachios, crushed, to decorate

For the custard

4 extra-large egg yolks

7 tablespoons/90g granulated sugar

1 teaspoon vanilla extract

1½ teaspoons rose water

3 tablespoons cornstarch

3⅓ cups/800ml whole milk

SERVES 6 TO 8

Place the water, sugar, cardamom, and lemon juice in a saucepan and bring to a boil. Add the pears and lower the heat to a simmer. Cook for 5 minutes, then carefully remove the fruit (or strain it in a sieve, making sure you retain the poaching liquid). Let cool on a plate.

Return the poaching liquid to the saucepan, add the dried apricots, and cook for 10 minutes over medium heat until they have softened. Remove the apricots and set them aside to cool. (Don't throw away the liquid though, we'll be using that later.)

Make the custard by whisking together the egg yolks, sugar, vanilla, rose water, and cornstarch in a large bowl until the mixture is pale and has doubled in size. Place the milk in a large saucepan and heat it to just below simmering point. Pour a ladleful of warm milk into the egg mixture and quickly whisk it in, then repeat with another ladle of milk until the mix loosens. Continue ladling all the milk in, whisking it as you do so.

Return the custard to the large pan and bring to a bare simmer, whisking gently as you cook for 5 minutes so it thickens. Let cool, whisking every few minutes so a skin doesn't form.

When completely cool, place a layer of ladyfingers in a serving dish and spoon ¼ cup/60ml of poaching liquid over the top. Top with a layer of the pears and dried apricots and finish by spooning another 5 tablespoons/75ml of poaching liquid over the fruit.

Carefully spoon an even layer of the cold custard over the fruit. Then cover the dish and refrigerate for least 1 hour. To serve, decorate with a handful of crushed pistachios, sprinkling them over the pudding.

Sour cherry cheesecake

Sour cherries are a prized ingredient in Turkey and here I've paired the sharp, tangy fruit with a baked yogurt and cream cheese cake. I use frozen sour cherries for this, as it's near-impossible to find them fresh in the UK and they have the added bonus of being pre-pitted, which saves time. (You can find them in the frozen aisles of natural food stores such as Whole Foods, or in Polish or Middle Eastern delis.) You can use sweet frozen cherries too, which are available in many supermarkets, you'll just need to decrease the amount of sugar in the topping by one-third. To reduce the risk of the cheesecake cracking, follow these tips carefully: don't over-mix the ingredients, be sure to line the baking pan, cook it slowly (if your oven runs hot, I'd be tempted to lower the temperature given below and cook it for a little longer), and let the cheesecake cool down very slowly. This needs to be made ahead of time, as it has to chill for at least four hours before serving. I use a 9-inch/23cm springform cake pan for this.

7 oz/200g graham crackers
7 tablespoons/100g unsalted
   butter, melted
1 lb 5 oz/600g full-fat cream
   cheese, room temperature
⅔ cup/200g strained full-fat
   Greek-style yogurt
1 cup/200g granulated sugar
3 extra-large eggs, lightly beaten
1 tablespoon all-purpose flour
1 tablespoon vanilla extract
1 teaspoon finely grated unwaxed
   lemon zest
1 tablespoon lemon juice

For the topping
14 oz/400g frozen, pitted sour
   cherries (see recipe
   introduction)
¾ cup/150g granulated sugar
1 tablespoon cornstarch

SERVES 8

Line a 9-inch/23cm springform cake pan with parchment paper. Put the graham crackers in a food processor and blitz to crumbs. Alternatively, place them in a plastic bag and hit them with a rolling pin until they are finely crushed (the latter is slightly more therapeutic).

Mix the crushed graham crackers with the melted butter, then spoon into the prepared pan, pressing down the bottom to form an even layer. (I sometimes use the bottom of a cup or glass to even out the crumb.) Transfer to the refrigerator to set.

Beat the cream cheese and yogurt until smooth. Whisk in the sugar, eggs, and flour, then the vanilla, lemon zest, and juice.

Preheat the oven to 325°F/160°C (and see recipe introduction). Pour the filling into the chilled graham cracker crust and bake for around 1 hour. You can tell it is cooked when it looks set but still has a wobble in the middle. Now turn off the oven, open its door and allow the cheesecake to cool for 10 minutes without touching it. Remove it from the oven and let cool completely, then chill for 4 hours.

To make the topping, place the frozen cherries and sugar in a saucepan over medium heat. Stir frequently to begin with, so the sugar doesn't catch. Once the cherries have defrosted and the sauce come to a boil, add the cornstarch and simmer for 5 minutes. Set aside and let cool.

To serve, either spoon the topping all over the cheesecake, or slice the cheesecake into pieces and place a dollop of cherries on top of each serving.

Turkish semolina halva

İRMİK HELVASI

There are dozens of different types of halva eaten across the Eastern Mediterranean and Middle East but, by my reckoning, this semolina version is the best. In Greece, I'd often be given a complimentary slice at the end of a meal in a restaurant, while in Turkey this is one of a series of dishes often made to honor those that have recently passed away. In either country, however, it is an easy, comforting, and quick treat to make, with the bonus that it fills your kitchen with a gorgeous toasted caramel and cinnamon scent. For the best results, use a wide-bottomed saucepan to give you plenty of surface area to toast the semolina. You can serve this warm or at room temperature, but whichever you choose, you'll probably want a cup of tea or coffee alongside it. This will last in an airtight container for about three days.

2 cups/480ml whole milk
1¼ cups/250g granulated sugar
1 cup/240ml water
1 teaspoon vanilla extract
½ teaspoon ground cinnamon, plus (optional, if serving warm) more to serve
3 tablespoons unsalted butter
6 tablespoons/90ml sunflower oil
1½ cups/250g semolina
¼ cup/30g pine nuts

MAKES 12 SERVINGS

Place the milk, sugar, and water in a saucepan over medium heat and gently stir until the sugar has completely dissolved. Take off the heat, add the vanilla and cinnamon, and set aside.

Place the butter and oil in a large, wide-bottomed saucepan over medium heat and stir until the butter has melted. Add the semolina and cook it for 10 minutes, stirring the whole time. The idea here is to slowly toast the grains so, over time, you'll see them darken in color.

After 10 minutes, add the pine nuts and cook for 8 minutes, stirring frequently so the semolina doesn't burn, until the mixture reaches a golden brown color.

Now, very carefully, pour the milk mixture into the semolina, standing back while you do this as it can splutter.

Decrease the heat to low and stir until the liquid has fully combined and the semolina has started to thicken. This will take 4 to 5 minutes. You can tell it is ready when the halva sticks together and comes away from the sides of pan.

To serve, you can scoop it into small bowls, dust with a little cinnamon, and serve warm. Or place it in a rectangular baking dish, flatten it down with the back of a spoon, let it cool, then cut it into diamonds or squares.

Candied pumpkin with tahini & date syrup

KABAK TATLISI

Candied pumpkin is a popular sweet in Turkey, where it can either be cooked on the stove or in an oven and then served plain as it is, or—for a fancier version—topped with *kaymak*, or tahini and date syrup. I've opted for the oven method here for ease and speed so, while you need to start this the night before you want to eat it, there is very little to do other than bake the pumpkin.

3⅓ lb/1.5kg sugar pumpkin, peeled, seeded, and cut into 2-inch/5cm wedges
2¼ cups/450g granulated sugar

To serve
tahini
date syrup
crushed walnuts

SERVES 6

Place the pumpkin or squash in a roasting dish and sprinkle with the sugar. Toss to ensure the pumpkin or squash is evenly coated, then let it rest for 30 minutes; after this time you should see that the sugar has begun to melt. Spoon this syrup back over the pumpkin or squash, then cover the dish with foil and let it rest on the work surface for at least 12 hours.

By the next day, the sugar should have completely dissolved and the pumpkin or squash will have released its juices.

Preheat the oven to 350°F/180°C.

Take off the foil and transfer the dish to the oven to bake for 1 hour, spooning the juices back over the pumpkin every 20 minutes. Remove from the oven and allow to cool completely in its dish.

To serve, place a pumpkin slice on a serving plate, drizzle with a couple of tablespoons of tahini and 1 tablespoon date syrup, and finish with a smattering of crushed walnuts.

Gulab jaman

These soft milk doughnuts steeped in cardamom and rose syrup are popular throughout Afghanistan and the Indian subcontinent and I'm including a recipe for them in this book in honor of all the Afghans I met in Lesvos. They can be served hot or at room temperature, just be sure to remove them from the refrigerator about 1 hour before you want to eat them, or stick them in the microwave. I highly recommend using a kitchen thermometer to measure the temperature of the oil you are frying them in, as it is crucial they are fried on relatively low heat (around 266°F/130°C) or you risk them browning quickly on the outside but not cooking all the way through. You can buy milk powder online, in Indian subcontinental grocery stores, or in the "world food" section of larger supermarkets.

For the syrup
3¼ cups/750ml water
2 cups/400g granulated sugar
¾ teaspoon ground green
    cardamom (from about 12 pods,
    seeds removed and ground)
1 tablespoon rose water

For the dough balls
2½ cups/250g milk powder
½ cup plus 1 tablespoon/70g
    all-purpose flour
1 tablespoon fine semolina
½ teaspoon baking powder
1 to 2 tablespoons ghee, melted
¾ cup to ¾ cup plus 2
    tablespoons/180–200ml
    lukewarm whole milk
1 quart/1 liter vegetable oil,
    for deep-frying
salt
crushed shelled, unsalted
    pistachios, to serve (optional)

MAKES AROUND 20
SERVES 8 TO 10

Begin by making a spice-infused syrup. For this, place the water, sugar, and cardamom in a large saucepan and bring to a boil. Keep the liquid at a rolling boil for about 10 minutes, stirring occasionally, until it thickens into a light syrup. Add the rose water, stir well, then take off the heat.

For the dough balls, place the milk powder, flour, semolina, and baking powder in a bowl with a pinch of salt. Add 1 tablespoon of the melted ghee, then slowly add the warm milk until you can form a smooth dough, lightly kneading it for a few minutes. (You may not need all the milk, so incorporate it gradually.) Use your hands to shape the dough into 20 equal-size balls about the size of a golf ball. If they start to look like they might crack, use a little more melted ghee to smooth them out.

Heat the vegetable oil in a heavy-bottomed saucepan over medium heat until it reaches 266°F/130°C on a cooking thermometer. Line a plate with paper towel, then carefully add the jamans to the oil in batches of 4 to 6 so you don't overcrowd the pan. Fry for 5 to 7 minutes until dark golden brown all over. Remove one to check they have cooked through—you want them firm and cake-like in the middle—and if they are not, cook for a few more minutes. Transfer to paper towel once they are done.

After you have cooked all the jamans and they have cooled a little, place them in the saucepan with the syrup and let soak for at least 6 hours, or overnight.

To serve, spoon them out of the syrup and place on a serving plate, with a few crushed pistachios on top, if you want. I like to eat these warm, so reheat them in a microwave, or in a saucepan, in some of their syrup.

Honey & ricotta cake
MELOPITA

This is inspired by my visit to Melissa, a refugee and migrant women's support center in Athens (see page 65), whose name means "honeybee" in Greek. Honey cakes are one of the oldest recorded recipes in Greek history and were traditionally offered up to the gods as thanks. This version combines thick, floral honey with soft local cheeses such as *anthotyros* or *mizithra*, but as those can be hard to source outside of Greece I've suggested substituting them with ricotta. You can serve this warm, as a soft pudding, or in a more traditional Greek fashion: cold with a black espresso on the side.

unsalted butter, for the pan
2⅔ cups/650g ricotta
½ cup plus 2 tablespoons/210g
   honey
1 teaspoon vanilla extract
1 teaspoon ground cinnamon
1 teaspoon finely grated
   unwaxed lemon zest
1 tablespoon lemon juice
3 extra-large eggs, lightly beaten
1 tablespoon cornstarch
salt

For the topping
6 tablespoons/130g honey
2 tablespoons thyme leaves
⅛ teaspoon ground cinnamon

SERVES 4 TO 6

Preheat the oven to 400°F/200°C.

Butter an 8-inch/20cm springform cake pan and line the bottom and sides with parchment paper.

Place the ricotta in a large bowl and add the honey, vanilla, cinnamon, lemon zest and juice, and a pinch of salt. Whisk the mixture until it is completely smooth and free of any lumps.

Add the eggs to the ricotta mixture along with the cornstarch and whisk again.

Spoon the batter into the prepared pan and bake for 50 to 60 minutes, or until the top of the cake has turned golden brown.

Meanwhile, heat the honey for the topping in a small saucepan with the thyme and cinnamon until it comes to a boil. Switch off the heat and allow the mixture to infuse.

When the cake is cooked, take it out of the oven and cool in the pan for 5 minutes, then gently transfer it to a serving plate. Reheat the infused honey until it has loosened up and is pourable, then spoon it over the cake.

You can either let it cool for 10 minutes and then serve it warm like a pudding, or leave it until it is completely set and firm, which will take at least 1 hour.

Fig & peach tart

This easy-to-assemble tart is the perfect vehicle for carrying two of the quintessential summer flavors of the Eastern Mediterranean: ripe figs and sweet peaches. It's a very forgiving recipe and you can play around with the flavorings and fruit you use. The amount of sugar is very much dependent on the sweetness of the fruit, so if yours is a bit on the under-ripe side, feel free to add more sugar to the filling. I like to serve this with whipped cream or *kaymak* and small dark cups of coffee.

For the pastry
2 cups/250g all-purpose flour, plus more to dust
¼ cup/45g granulated sugar
¼ teaspoon salt
½ cup plus 2 tablespoons/150g cold unsalted butter, finely chopped
1 extra-large egg yolk (reserve the white for the glaze)
1 tablespoon cold water

For the filling
2 ripe and sweet small peaches (total weight about 11 oz/320g)
5 ripe figs
1 teaspoon vanilla extract
½ teaspoon ground cinnamon
1 tablespoon lemon juice
½ cup/110g demerara sugar
3 tablespoons cornstarch

For the glaze
1 extra-large egg white, lightly beaten
2 tablespoons demerara sugar

SERVES 4 TO 6

To make the pastry, place the flour, granulated sugar, salt, and butter in a large bowl and rub them all together with your fingertips and palms until they resemble breadcrumbs. Lightly beat the egg yolk and the cold water, then add this to the bowl, using your hands to lightly knead everything together into a soft ball of dough. Wrap in plastic wrap and transfer to the refrigerator for 1 hour.

When you are ready to start baking, preheat the oven to 400°F/200°C.

Slice the peaches into ¾-inch/2cm-thick slices, removing the pits, and quarter the figs. Place the fruit in a bowl and toss with the vanilla, cinnamon, lemon juice, demerara sugar, and cornstarch.

Place a sheet of parchment paper on a work surface and put the ball of pastry on it. Lightly flour a rolling pin and use it to roll out the pastry into a circle around ¼ inch/5mm thick and 14 inches/35cm in diameter. Don't worry if the edges are rough, and if the pastry starts coming apart that's no problem either, just squish it together with your fingers. Place the parchment paper with the dough on a baking sheet.

Now arrange the peach and fig slices in the center of the circle, leaving a 2-inch/5cm border. You can do this by piling them all into the middle, or making a pattern such as concentric circles. Once you are done, fold the edges of the pastry over the fruit. Use your fingers to bring the pastry together where you have gaps. Finally use a pastry brush to lightly coat the top of the pastry with the beaten egg white, then sprinkle the crust with demerara sugar.

Bake for around 40 minutes, until the top of the pastry is an even dark golden-brown color. You can serve this warm, but I think the flavors improve at room temperature, so I let it cool for 30 minutes.

Bougatsa

This is my favorite Greek pastry, filled with smooth vanilla and semolina custard and dusted with lots of confectioners' sugar and cinnamon. It is often eaten for breakfast, though I think it works well at any time of day when you want a pick-me-up and, while a black coffee on the side isn't essential, I do think it complements it very well. Serve warm or at room temperature and make sure you cut it when it is out of the pan, as it's much easier that way.

For the custard
2 tablespoons unsalted butter, plus
　　more, melted, for the pan
3¼ cup/750ml whole milk
¾ cup/150g granulated sugar
1½ teaspoons vanilla extract
½ cup/85g fine semolina
2-inch/5cm strip of unwaxed
　　lemon peel
2 extra-large eggs, lightly beaten
salt

For the pastry
8 to 12 sheets of filo pastry,
　　depending on the size of the pan
5 tablespoons/70g unsalted butter,
　　melted

To serve
about ¼ cup/30g confectioners'
　　sugar
1 teaspoon ground cinnamon

SERVES 6

Line a medium-size baking pan with parchment paper and brush it with some melted butter. I use a 9 x 13-inch/23 x 33 cm pan, but you could use an 8-inch/20cm cake pan, too. You'll be cutting the bougatsa into small pieces anyway and wrapping the filo around a set custard, so the shape of the pan you use is pretty forgiving.

Place the milk in a large saucepan over medium heat and bring it to a simmer. Add the butter, sugar, and vanilla and stir occasionally until the sugar has melted. Add the semolina and strip of lemon peel and cook for 5 minutes until thickened, whisking every minute so the custard stays smooth. Take off the heat and let cool for 10 minutes.

Preheat the oven to 375°F/190°C. Unroll the first sheet of filo and place it in the prepared pan with about ¾ inch/2cm overhanging. Brush this sheet with melted butter, then layer another sheet of filo on to it. Repeat until you have 6 layers.

By now, the custard should have cooled considerably. Remove the strip of lemon peel and whisk in the beaten eggs and a pinch of salt, stirring well to ensure they don't curdle. Then gently pour this custard into the filo pastry and use the back of a spoon or a spatula to smooth it out. (It will smell delicious and you are allowed to eat a sneaky spoonful or so yourself.)

Fold any overhanging filo sheets into the middle of the pan (it will cover some of the custard) and start layering the top of the pie with more filo, using the same technique of placing a sheet on top and then buttering it. Use large sheets to do this, so you can tuck them down the sides. Repeat to make 6 layers. Bake for around 25 minutes, until golden and crispy.

Allow to cool for 10 minutes, then carefully remove the pie from the pan and place it on a serving plate. Use a sharp knife to slice it into 1½-inch/4cm squares or segments, then very generously dust with the confectioners' sugar and cinnamon.

Chocolate, orange, & olive oil mousse

Citrus fruits are such an iconic feature of the Cypriot landscape that I left the island wanting to incorporate their fragrances and flavors into as many dishes as possible. This dairy-free mousse is one of the results of that exploration, adapted from a recipe by Nigella Lawson in her book *At My Table*. The fragrant orange melds perfectly with the bitter chocolate and peppery olive oil create a silky, luscious mousse that tastes a bit like a Terry's Chocolate Orange. Only much better. If you like Cointreau, you might want to add a drop of that at the end, too.

6 oz/170g dark chocolate (70% cocoa solids), roughly chopped
5 tablespoons/75ml extra-virgin olive oil, plus more to serve
1 teaspoon finely grated unwaxed orange zest, plus more to serve
1 teaspoon cocoa powder, sifted
4 extra-large eggs, separated
¼ cup/50g granulated sugar
2 tablespoons orange juice
salt
sea salt flakes (optional)

SERVES 6

Melt the chocolate by placing it in a heatproof bowl above a saucepan of boiling water (don't let the bowl touch the water), or in a microwave. Once it has melted, let it cool for a few minutes, then stir in the olive oil, orange zest, cocoa powder, and ¼ teaspoon salt.

Whisk the egg yolks and sugar together in a separate bowl until they are pale and have almost doubled in volume.

In another, larger bowl, whisk the egg whites with a pinch of salt until you have stiff peaks.

Now, slowly pour the chocolate mixture into the beaten yolks and gently fold to mix it in. Add the orange juice and fold again.

Spoon in the beaten egg whites, one-third at a time, and keep folding the mousse together until you have no streaks.

Carefully spoon the mousse into 6 ramekins. Refrigerate these for at least 1 hour, then let them come to room temperature just before serving.

To serve, drizzle with some extra-virgin olive oil, a sprinkle of orange zest, and some sea salt flakes, if you like.

Raspberry & pomegranate roulade

If you've got a sweet tooth, you'll enjoy the dessert parlors of Cyprus. They are dotted throughout the island and feature shelves full of traditional and modern cakes and desserts, all adorned with local seasonal fruits, such as sour cherries, strawberries, figs, and pomegranates. In Famagusta, I lost my mind at one of these places and ordered four different desserts to try in one sitting and this is my version of a meringue I ate there. Assemble this close to the time you are eating it and save the egg yolks for making a custard such as the version in the *Charlotta* (see page 260).

For the meringue
4 extra-large egg whites
1 cup plus 2 tablespoons/225g
    granulated sugar
½ cup/50g almond meal
1 teaspoon lemon juice
1 teaspoon cornstarch

For the filling
1½ cups/350ml heavy cream
scant ⅔ cup/160g strained full-fat
    Greek-style yogurt
finely grated zest of
    1 unwaxed lemon
2 teaspoons lemon juice
1 teaspoon vanilla extract
2 tablespoons confectioners'
    sugar, plus more to dust
¾ cup/100g raspberries or
    strawberries
¾ cup/130g pomegranate seeds

For the topping
1 to 2 tablespoons shelled,
    unsalted pistachios,
    roughly chopped
    or crushed

SERVES 6 TO 8

Line a baking sheet with parchment paper and preheat the oven to 325°F/170°C. Place the egg whites in a large bowl and whisk to soft peaks. Slowly add the sugar, whisking in a few tablespoons at a time until it has all been incorporated and you have a stiff, glossy meringue. Add the almond meal, lemon juice, and cornstarch and gently fold in.

Spoon the meringue onto the parchment paper and use a spatula to spread it into a rectangular shape roughly 12 x 8 inches/ 30 x 20cm. Bake for 30 minutes until firm on top and slightly golden. Meanwhile, tear off another piece of parchment paper of the same size and lay it out on a clean work surface (you'll need this to roll your meringue when it's cooked).

Whisk the cream, yogurt, lemon zest, lemon juice, vanilla extract, and confectioners' sugar in a bowl to a thick cream. Place the berries in a bowl and use a fork to mash half, to create pools of juice.

When the meringue is cooked, lift the parchment on which it has been baking off the sheet and turn it crust side down on to the fresh piece of parchment paper you prepared earlier. Gently peel the parchment from the bottom of the meringue and allow it to completely cool (this will take about 10 minutes).

When the meringue is cold, spoon the cream over it, reserving a couple of tablespoons for decoration. Sprinkle with most of the pomegranate seeds, reserving 2 spoonsful for decoration, and scatter with berries, swirling the juices with the end of a spoon so you have bright pink streaks running through it.

Use the parchment paper to roll up the meringue as tightly as you can and transfer it to a serving dish. Use the remaining cream to create a strip along the roulade and scatter with the reserved pomegranate seeds and the pistachios. Chill for at least 30 minutes. Lightly dust with confectioners' sugar before serving.

Date & walnut brownies

Dates and walnuts are a common sweet pairing throughout the Eastern Mediterranean and these brownies are a more indulgent, dense, and chewy twist on that classic pairing. To get a crisper top on your chocolate brownie, while keeping the center soft, I suggest placing the baking pan in ice-cold water as soon as it comes out of the oven. This is optional, but I think it works.

7 oz/200g dark chocolate
    (70% cocoa solids), broken
1 cup plus 2 tablespoons/250g
    unsalted butter, softened
1 cup/200g granulated sugar
3 extra-large eggs, lightly beaten
½ cup/65g all-purpose flour, sifted
¾ cup/60g cocoa powder, sifted
½ teaspoon baking powder
¼ teaspoon salt
5¼ oz/150g medjool or Iranian
    dates, pitted and roughly
    chopped
1 cup/100g walnuts, chopped

MAKES ABOUT 16

Preheat the oven to 350°F/180°C. Line a 9-inch/23cm square or equivalent size baking pan with parchment paper.

Place a bowl over a pot of simmering water (make sure the bottom of the bowl does not touch the water) and add the chocolate. Allow it to melt, stirring occasionally, then remove from the heat immediately. (Be careful not to get any water or steam onto the chocolate as it will make it split!)

Beat the butter and sugar together until light and fluffy. I use a stand mixer, but you can do it by hand with some elbow grease. Gradually add the eggs, beating well between each addition to ensure they are thoroughly incorporated before pouring in any more. Fold in the melted chocolate, followed by the sifted flour, cocoa powder, baking powder, and salt. Finally stir in the chopped dates and walnuts.

Spoon the mixture into an even layer in the pan and bake for 20 to 25 minutes. Test with a toothpick: it should come out sticky, but not coated with the raw batter. If it does, put it back into the oven for another few minutes.

Fill a large dish with ice and cold water and, when the brownies come out of the oven, place the baking pan in this water bath, without letting any water run onto the brownies. Let cool in the ice water, then cut into rectangles or squares to serve.

A WORLD
WITHOUT BORDERS
NICOSIA, CYPRUS

In ancient Greek mythology, the island of Cyprus is associated with Aphrodite, the goddess of love and beauty. Legend has it that she was born out of the sea foam in the waters around Cyprus, at a place which today is marked by Aphrodite's Rock, a stack that majestically emerges from the sea in the southern part of the island. Ancient Greek myths also say that it was here, on this island, that Aphrodite planted the very first pomegranate, a fruit long held as a symbol of fertility and beauty throughout the Middle East.

Today the pomegranate continues to be celebrated across Cyprus, with villages in the Turkish Cypriot North and Greek Cypriot South holding annual festivals to commemorate its splendor with fêtes, foods, and artisan handicrafts. Pomegranates are not the only point of connection on this divided island, but the reverence in which they are held by all who live here is a small symbol that—at least on some levels—the two communities are not as culturally different as their political leaders would have us believe.

The story of Cyprus feels to me like a microcosm of how man-made borders create xenophobia, division, and conflict. Throughout the last few thousand years, Cyprus's position at the nautical crossroads of the Eastern Mediterranean has meant that many empires and invaders have sought to have a stake here. Occupations by the Greeks, Egyptians, Persians, Romans, Byzantines, Arabs, Crusaders, Venetians, Ottomans, and the British (from whom Cyprus only gained independence in 1960) have all left their mark.

The legacy of all these empires is evident in the country's food culture; a rich tapestry of Mediterranean and Middle Eastern ingredients. As well as the ubiquitous pomegranate, ingredients such as tahini, carob, rose water, and grape molasses are commonplace, along with spices such as cumin, cinnamon, and coriander and the abundant use of fresh and dried herbs. This mix of influences has given Cyprus a diverse culinary catalog from which to draw, no doubt adding to the culture of an island that is overwhelmingly warm, hospitable, generous, family-oriented, and communal.

There are some particularly Cypriot culinary specialties however, such as the world-renowned Cypriot potato, a product of the island's rich red soil, which makes the best fries you will ever eat. And halloumi, the semi-hard brined cheese made from goat and sheep milk, which is arguably the island's most famous export. Or *loukanika*, spiced sausages flavored with red wine, orange zest, and fennel seeds, perfect for grilling on a barbecue. And I have a particular soft spot for the Cypriot way of cooking beans with wild greens. On the surface they are simple, dressed only with olive oil and lemon, but when assembled with Cypriot essentials—thick slices of sweet tomatoes, a bowl of olives, raw onion, and a wedge of bread—they are elevated to an elegant feast.

But these treasures sit against a troubled political backdrop. For this beautiful island is currently split into two: the Republic of Cyprus in the south and the Turkish Republic of Northern Cyprus (TRNC) in the north. The TRNC is currently only recognized as a state by Turkey, and considered by the United Nations to be occupied Cypriot territory. Both territories count Nicosia as their capital city.

This division is a relatively recent phenomenon. At the time of independence from the British, Greek Cypriots and Turkish Cypriots were equally dispersed around the country, living alongside each other. In the years leading up to independence, however, ethnic divisions between the two groups grew, stoked in part by the "divide and rule" tactics of the British, and amplified by regional power plays between the Greek Orthodox Church and the Greek government, who started campaigning for the island to be unified with Greece, something the Turkish government vehemently opposed.

After the British left, a power-sharing government between the two communities was formed, but tensions continued to amplify. In 1974, the Cypriot National Guard deposed the prime minister in a coup d'état, replacing him with a politician who was pro-unification with Greece. In response, Turkey invaded the island, to protect the Turkish Cypriot minority.

A civil war followed, after which the island was divided and there was a painful forced population exchange. Many Cypriots died during this conflict, others became refugees within their own island, many more were left traumatized by what took place, the legacy of which continues to be felt today. In order to keep the peace, a United Nations Buffer Zone, patrolled by a UN peacekeeping force, was established, to separate the two territories and the city of Nicosia. It is still in place today. The border remained closed

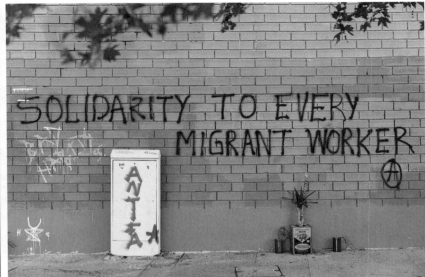

for thirty years, until 2004 when land crossings were allowed for the first time. That same year, a UN peace plan was developed, aiming to unite Cyprus, and was voted on in a referendum by all the island's inhabitants. The majority of Turkish Cypriots voted in favor of the plan, but most Greek Cypriots voted against. Today, the island remains divided.

I start my journey in Nicosia, where the food markets, restaurants, and cafés tell the story of the island's mixed culinary influences. With a *frappe* in hand—a quintessentially Cypriot version of iced coffee—I wander back and forth across the two sides of the city, snacking on the sweet, flaky tahini pastries called *tahinopitas*, or squares of *börek* filled with ground lamb and scattered with *pul biber*. Frequently I stop to buy from stalls that heave with summer's bounty, sometimes a bag of sour cherries, or fresh almonds, local avocados, watermelons of all sizes, and more ripe figs than even I could devour.

But while the food highlights similarities on both sides of the Green Line, the economic disparity between them is stark. Southern Cyprus has all the hallmarks of an economically successful European country, with developed infrastructure and booming tourism. Northern Cyprus, on the other hand, remains isolated and under-developed, a direct result of decades' worth of economic and trading sanctions against the country. As the days go on, spending my money in the Northern part of the island becomes more of a priority for me.

During my travels around Cyprus I stay on both sides of the island, exploring its exquisite coastlines, with turquoise-blue waters that—in the peak of summer—feel like you've stepped into a warm bath; and the rugged inland mountains, with their bougainvillea-lined villages, home to packs of cats that roam the alleys looking for kitchen scraps. I learn how to make halloumi from scratch with Greek Cypriot grandmothers, meet with members of a cross-border cycling club who are working together to develop group rides between the two communities, and am welcomed into family homes for traditional Sunday lunches of roast lamb *kleftiko* and *charlotta* milk pudding.

But amid the beauty and natural splendor, there are many moments when the reality of the cultural tensions is exposed and that leave me feeling uneasy. One Greek Cypriot woman, full of warmth and generosity, takes me out to lunch in Limassol, where we feast on braised lamb with okra, the local specialty of *gemista* (rice-stuffed onions and peppers), and crisp fried whitebait. She tells me stories of Cypriot history and speaks movingly of her childhood and becoming a refugee, when, after the civil war, her family had to flee their home in the Northern city of Famagusta. Then she mentions that now, when she goes to visit the Turkish side, she always takes her own food, as she does not trust the hygiene standards of places in the North and also feels that it isn't right that she should give "them" any money, as "they" should not be there. And while I understand the history of her opinions, it makes me frustrated that such casual racism against a whole group of people can exist and, as she speaks, I think of all the Cypriots I've met who want to identify as neither Turk nor Greek, but as just that: Cypriot.

Other examples are more entertaining. Such as the British man, married to a Greek-Cypriot woman, who warns me, "Be careful about crossing the border to the North, it's not safe over there." Before I have the chance to ask him why, he starts a rant about the Turkish presence on this island and how he'd once got into an argument with a Turkish Cypriot border official who had stopped him driving across because of outstanding speeding fines. Enraged, the man's cheeks turn scarlet as he tells me that the border official asked him to turn back and how he had shouted back at the Turkish Cypriot border official, "You go back!" I bite my lip, trying not to laugh at the ludicrous premise of a British man living in Cyprus telling Cypriots to "go back" anywhere. I guess old colonial tendencies don't wear off so easily . . .

Then there are the young Greek Cypriot eco-activists, whom I meet for drinks in a central Nicosia square. Over rose-infused cordials we speak about climate justice, seed sovereignty, and the farming perils of multinational corporations, common ground in which we are all interested. Then I ask them about any cross-border initiatives with the North . . . and wait as my question drops like a stone into an awkward silence. They tell me they have never been to the Turkish North. I ask why, and another silence ensues; they simply don't feel comfortable because of what happened to their grandparents' villages. At this, I point out to them that we are sitting only around three hundred yards from the pedestrian border crossing which I had passed through twice already that day and ask what is to stop us all from going over later that evening? They smile wryly and gulp down their drinks.

"I hate the separated island," Çizge tells me, as she rolls out pastry to make her specialty, a vegan mushroom *börek*. "These days I try not to think about it more than I have to. It just really gets me down." I'd come to join Çizge Yalkın and her grandmother, Nahide Köşkeroğlu, in a village just north of Nicosia, to learn how to make some Cypriot dishes such as stuffed zucchini flowers and hear more about the impact of the separation on everyday lives. "We used to live side-by-side with each other," Nahide tells me as she begins assembling

ingredients to make a halloumi and olive bread. "My father had a best friend who was Greek. We would go to their weddings, they would come to ours, there was no difference, we were always brothers and sisters." I nod and watch her measure flour into a bowl and slowly pour in olive oil. "We just wanted to live in peace," she continues, "but the people at the top didn't get that." She shakes her head in disgust. "To hell with all of them."

Nahide tells me of how her family had been forcibly displaced, first as a result of the Greeks driving them from their village in the 1950s, then, after the Turkish invasion and subsequent civil war in the 1970s, again they had to leave their home, this time in Nicosia. "Our fanatics and their fanatics are the same," she tells me, visibly channeling her anger into kneading the bread dough. "I just wish the island could merge and turn into something different, coming together as an island of Cypriots, because that's what we all are."

In my final days in Cyprus, my favorite place to spend my time is the café at Home for Co-operation, a social space operating out of a building within the UN Green Line buffer zone. The café is situated, literally, in no man's land, making it a neutral space and—because of that—a place for everybody. It was created by activists who wanted to promote civil society and dialogue beyond the constraints of the official political divides, and a space where Greek and Turkish Cypriots could meet, socialize, organize, and—crucially—eat. As one of the staff remarks, "I have no doubt that Cyprus will unite one day, and I hope for that. But I don't think it will come from up high, because some leaders signed a piece of paper. Unity is only going to be possible by our communities coming together to build bridges. It'll come from us."

Each time I visit, the café is always full, bustling with conversation and optimism, fed in part by the delicious food—taro stew, souvlaki, citrus cakes—but also by their vision of another world. A world where the construct of a territorial line arbitrarily dividing communities from each other does not exist. A world where we honor the differences in our cultural backgrounds, but understand that we are all equals living on one shared planet. A world in which the place where you are born does not determine the opportunities you are given. A world where you are free to move, work, travel, and live wherever you please and be welcomed there as a fellow member of the human race.

A world without borders.

Menu ideas

Quick & easy weeknight meals
Smoky lima beans 112
Lentils with preserved lemons & zhoug 130
Turkish bride soup 182
Istanbul's famous mackerel sandwiches 214
Sea bream with pistachio & herb smash 217
Fish kebabs with skordalia 218

Eastern Mediterranean picnic
Olive bread 75
Tomato & mint dolma 81
Spinach, herb, & feta pie 86
Taramasalata 103
Zucchini & feta fritters 125
Cypriot potato salad 152
Tomato & za'atar salad 156

Autumn/winter dinner
Greek greens 101
Hot yogurt & spinach soup 184
Beef stifado 243
Chocolate, orange, & olive oil mousse 274

Spring/summer dinner
Orzo rice 79
Turkish shepherd's salad 148
Pomegranate & sumac chicken 230
Raspberry & pomegranate roulade 277

Eid
Orzo rice 79
Afghan spiced pumpkin 115
Classic Turkish meatballs 240
Gulab jaman 268

Easter lunch
Arugula, mushroom, & kefalotyri salad 161
Mushroom moussaka 210, or Lamb shank
    kleftiko 235
Pear, apricot, & rose water pudding 260

Vegan dinner
Turkish white beans 108
Stuffed roasted eggplants 116
Broccolini with red peppers & dill 118
Candied pumpkin with tahini
    & date syrup 266

Greek mezze for 4
Almost fava 110
Halloumi saganaki 122
Greek salad 146
Greek tomato meatballs 244
Bread & olives

Turkish mezze for 4
Garlicky eggplant salad 99
Turkish white beans 108
Zucchini & feta fritters 125
Turkish shepherd's salad 148
Spicy bulgur in lettuce cups 155
Bread & olives

Dairy-free, gluten-free, & vegan recipe index

Dairy-free

Breakfast
Sour cherry jam 50
Apricot jam 50

Breads & grains
Turkish flatbread 72
Olive bread 75
Pita bread 78
Tomato & mint dolma 81

Mezze, light meals, & sides
Spicy red pepper & walnut smash 100
Greek greens 101
Turkish white beans 108
Almost fava 110
Smoky lima beans 112
Stuffed roast eggplants 116
Broccolini with
    red peppers & dill 118
Greek vegetable medley 128
Lentils with preserved lemons & zhoug 130
Sardines in grape leaves 131
Pickled red cabbage 132

Salads
Turkish shepherd's salad 148
Cypriot potato salad 152
Spicy bulgur in lettuce cups 155
Tomato & za'atar salad 156
Grilled onion salad with pomegranate
    & sumac 160
Crunchy winter slaw 162
Beet, fennel, & pomegranate salad 165
Ezme salad 166

Soups
Pumpkin & cardamom soup 190

Mains
Black-eyed peas with chard 206
Chana masala 209
Tagliatelle with herbed lentils 212

Istanbul's famous mackerel sandwiches 214
Sea bream with pistachio & herb smash 217
Herb & paprika chicken 224
Pomegranate & sumac chicken 230
Rakhine chicken curry 232
Classic Turkish meatballs 240
Beef stifado 243
Greek tomato meatballs 244

Desserts
Candied pumpkin with tahini
    & date syrup 266

Gluten-free

Breakfast
Griddled fruits, yogurt, & honey 46
Sour cherry jam 50
Apricot jam 50
Fragrant oats with rose water 55
Eggs with yogurt & chile butter 56
Spiced tomato scramble 59

Breads & grains
Tomato & mint dolma 81

Mezze, light meals, & sides
Garlicky eggplant salad 99
Spicy red pepper & walnut smash 100
Greek greens 101
Iranian eggplant & kashk dip 105
Yogurt drink 106
Yogurt with cucumber & mint 107
Turkish white beans 108
Almost fava 110
Smoky lima beans 112
Afghan spiced pumpkin 115
Stuffed roasted eggplants 116
Broccolini with
    red peppers & dill 118
Turkish braised carrots & leeks 121

Charred cabbage with hazelnuts
   & chile butter 126
Greek vegetable medley 128
Lentils with preserved lemons & zhoug 130
Sardines in grape leaves 131
Pickled red cabbage 132

Salads
Greek salad 146
Turkish shepherd's salad 148
Sweet potato, chickpea, & tahini salad 151
Cypriot potato salad 152
Tomato & za'atar salad 156
Sunshine salad 158
Grilled onion salad with pomegranate
   & sumac 160
Arugula, mushroom, & kefalotyri
   salad 161
Crunchy winter slaw 162
Beet, fennel, & pomegranate salad 165
Ezme salad 166

Soups
Hot yogurt & spinach soup 184
Spiced carrot soup 187
Lemon chicken soup 189
Pumpkin & cardamom soup 190

Mains
Chana masala 209
Fish kebabs with skordalia 218
Prawn saganaki 220
Herb & paprika chicken 224
Pomegranate & sumac chicken 230
Rakhine chicken curry 232
Lamb shank kleftiko 235
Adana kebabs 237

Desserts
Candied pumpkin with tahini
   & date syrup 266
Honey & ricotta cake 269
Chocolate, orange, & olive oil mousse 274
Raspberry & pomegranate roulade 277

Vegan

Breakfast
Sour cherry jam 50
Apricot jam 50

Breads & grains
Olive bread 75
Pita bread 78
Tomato & mint dolma 81

Mezze, light meals, & sides
Spicy red pepper & walnut smash 100
Greek greens 101
Turkish white beans 108
Almost fava 110
Smoky lima beans 112
Stuffed roasted eggplants 116
Broccolini with red peppers & dill 118
Greek vegetable medley 128
Lentils with preserved lemons &
   zhoug 130
Pickled red cabbage 132

Salads
Turkish shepherd's salad 148
Cypriot potato salad 152
Spicy bulgur in lettuce cups 155
Grilled onion salad with pomegranate
   & sumac 160
Beet, fennel, & pomegranate salad 165
Ezme salad 166

Soups
Pumpkin & cardamom soup 190

Mains
Black-eyed peas with chard 206
Chana masala 209
Tagliatelle with herbed lentils 212

Desserts
Candied pumpkin with tahini & date
   syrup 266

Index

A

Abdul 140
adana kebabs 237
AD.DAR 196, 212
Afghan refugees 105, 115, 174, 177–8, 268
Afghan spiced pumpkin 115
Aleppo, Syria 100, 212
Alozon, Yousef 196
Altinoglou, Lena 138–43
Ama Laxei 65
Aphrodite 283
apples: beet, fennel, & pomegranate salad 165
apricots
   apricot jam 50
   pear, apricot, & rose water pudding 260
arugula
   arugula, mushroom, & kefalotyri salad 161
   sunshine salad 158
Athens, Greece 37–40, 65, 257
avocados 158
   sunshine salad 158

B

bamboo shoots: Rakhine chicken curry 232
beef
   beef stifado 243
   classic Turkish meatballs 240–1
   Greek tomato meatballs 244
beet
   beet, fennel, & pomegranate salad 165
   lentils with preserved lemons & zhoug 130
black-eyed peas with chard 206
Blue Zones 91
Bosporus strait 195, 214, 249
Bougainvillea Guesthouse 84
bougatsa 257, 272
bread 71
   cardamom egg toast 54
   delicious things on toast 48–51
   Istanbul's famous mackerel sandwiches 214
   olive bread 75
   pita bread 78
   spiced cornbread with feta 76
   taramasalata 103
   Turkish flatbread 72
breakfast 42–63
Breakfast at the Park 68
broccoli: Broccolini with red peppers & dill 118
Broccolini with red peppers & dill 118
brownies, date & walnut 278
bulgur wheat
   spicy bulgur in lettuce cups 155
   Turkish bride soup 182
butter 29–30
   charred cabbage with hazelnuts & chile butter 126
   eggs with yogurt & chile butter 56

C

cabbage
   charred cabbage with hazelnuts & chile butter 126
   crunchy winter slaw 162
   pickled red cabbage 132
cakes
   citrus cake 258
   date & walnut brownies 278
   honey & ricotta cake 269
candied pumpkin with tahini & date syrup 266
capers
   Cypriot potato salad 152
   Greek salad 146
   sardines in grape leaves 131
   tomato & za'atar salad 156
cardamom
   cardamom egg toast 54
   pumpkin & cardamom soup 190
carrots
   crunchy winter slaw 162
   spiced carrot soup 187
   Turkish braised carrots & leeks 121
chana masala 209
chard
   black-eyed peas with chard 206
   Greek greens 101
   spinach, herb, & feta pie 86
charred cabbage with hazelnuts & chile butter 126
cheese 29–30, 161, 284
   arugula, mushroom, & kefalotyri salad 161
   Greek salad 146
   halloumi & mint muffins 84
   halloumi saganaki 122
   mushroom moussaka 210
   prawn saganaki 220
   spiced cornbread with feta 76
   spinach, herb, & feta pie 86
   sunshine salad 158
   zucchini & feta fritters 125
   see also cream cheese; ricotta
cheesecake, sour cherry 263
cherries
   sour cherry cheesecake 263
   sour cherry jam 50
chicken
   herb & paprika chicken 224
   lemon chicken soup 189
   pomegranate & sumac chicken 230
   Rakhine chicken curry 232
   veiled rice with spiced chicken 227–8
chickpeas
   chana masala 209
   sweet potato, chickpea, & tahini salad 151
chocolate
   chocolate, orange, & olive oil mousse 274
   date & walnut brownies 278
Christopoulou, Nadina 66–8

cilantro
  Greek greens 101
  lentils with preserved lemons
    & zhoug 130
citrus fruit 258, 274
  citrus cake 258
Çiya Sofrasi 250
coconut milk: pumpkin &
    cardamom soup 190
cod's roe: taramasalata 103
cornbread: spiced cornbread with
    feta 76
cream 29–30
  raspberry & pomegranate
    roulade 277
cream cheese
  citrus cake 258
  sour cherry cheesecake 263
crunchy winter slaw 162
cucumber
  Greek salad 146
  spicy bulgur in lettuce cups 155
  Turkish shepherd's salad 148
  yogurt with cucumber & mint
    107
Culinary Backstreets 65
curry, Rakhine chicken 232
custard
  bougatsa 272
  pear, apricot, & rose water
    pudding 260
Cypriot potato salad 152
Cyprus 22, 43, 258, 277, 283–4
  breakfasts 43
  citrus fruits 258, 274
  pantry ingredients 29–31
  political history 27, 283, 284–7,
    288–91
  vegetables 145
  see also individual towns

D
Dadar 172
Dağdeviren, Musa 250–5
date & walnut brownies 278
date syrup 31
  candied pumpkin with tahini
    & date syrup 266
desserts 256–81

dill, Broccolini with red peppers &
    118
dips
  almost fava 110
  Iranian eggplant & kashk dip
    105–6
  spicy red pepper & walnut smash
    100
  taramasalata 103
Doctors without Borders 172
dolma, tomato & mint 81–2
Doriti, Carolina 65
doughnuts: gulab jaman 268
drink, yogurt 106
Duguid, Naomi 232

E
eggplants
  garlicky eggplant salad 99
  Greek vegetable medley 128
  Iranian eggplant & kashk dip
    105–6
  mushroom moussaka 210
  stuffed roasted eggplants 116
eggs
  cardamom egg toast 54
  chocolate, orange, & olive oil
    mousse 274
  eggs with yogurt & chile butter 56
  raspberry & pomegranate
    roulade 277
  spiced tomato scramble 59
  sujuk & eggs 60
  zucchini & feta fritters 125
Erdoğan, Melda 227, 249, 250
Exarcheia, Athens 37–8
ezme salad 166
Ezo 182

F
Famagusta, Cyprus 277, 288
Farnaz 172
fava, almost 110
fennel: beet, fennel, &
    pomegranate salad 165
feta cheese 30
  Greek salad 146
  prawn saganaki 220
  spiced cornbread with feta 76

spinach, herb, & feta pie 86
  zucchini & feta fritters 125
figs 37, 40, 43
  fig & peach tart 271
  halloumi saganaki 122
filo pastry
  bougatsa 272
  spinach, herb, & feta pie 86
fish
  fish kebabs with skordalia 218
  Istanbul's famous mackerel
    sandwiches 214
  sardines in grape leaves 131
  sea bream with pistachio & herb
    smash 217
flatbread, Turkish 72
fragrant oats with rose water 55
fritters, zucchini & feta 125
fruit 258, 274
  griddled fruits, yogurt, & honey 46
  see also individual types of fruit
fruit molasses 31

G
garlic
  garlicky eggplant salad 99
  lamb shank kleftiko 235–6
  steamed garlic & chile mussels
    223
Göçer, Berrak 199–203
graham crackers: sour cherry
    cheesecake 263
grape leaves
  sardines in grape leaves 131
  tomato & mint dolma 81–2
grape molasses 31
  grape molasses & tahini on
    toast 48
Greece 22, 27
  breakfasts 43
  pantry ingredients 29–31
  vegetables 145
  see also individual cities
    & islands
Greek greens 101
Greek salad 145, 146
Greek tomato meatballs 244
Greek vegetable medley 128
greens, Greek 101

gulab jaman 268
Gulf of Yera, Greece 172

H
halloumi 30, 284
    halloumi & mint muffins 84
    halloumi saganaki 122
    sunshine salad 158
halva, Turkish semolina 264
Hatice Anne 76
hazelnuts 126
    charred cabbage with hazelnuts
        & chile butter 126
herbs 30
    herb & paprika chicken 224
    pistachio & herb sauce 217
    spinach, herb, & feta pie 86
    tagliatelle with herbed lentils
        212
Home For All 172, 174–8
Home for Co-operation 258, 291
honey
    griddled fruits, yogurt, & honey 46
    honey & ricotta cake 269
    kaymak, honey, & walnuts on
        toast 48

I
Ikaria, Greece 91–4, 128, 145
ingredients 29–31
Iranian eggplant & kashk dip 105–6
Istanbul, Turkey 97, 187, 195–203,
    212, 214, 249–55
Istanbul's famous mackerel
    sandwiches 214
Izmir, Turkey 244

J
jams 48–50
    apricot jam 50
    sour cherry jam 50

K
kale
    Greek greens 101
    lemon chicken soup 189
Kamara 172
kashk: Iranian eggplant & kashk dip
    105–6

Katsouris, Katerina 171–2, 174,
    177, 178
Katsouris, Nikos 171–2
kaymak 30
    kaymak, honey, & walnuts on
        toast 48
kebabs 205
    adana kebabs 237
    fish kebabs with skordalia 218
kefalotyri 161
    arugula, mushroom, & kefalotyri
        salad 161
    mushroom moussaka 210
kleftiko, lamb shank 235–6
Klephts 235
Köşkeroğlu, Nahide 81, 288–91
Kurds 200–3, 252

L
lamb
    Greek tomato meatballs 244
    lamb shank kleftiko 235–6
leeks, Turkish braised carrots & 121
lemons
    lemon chicken soup 189
    lentils with preserved lemons
        & zhoug 130
lentils
    lentils with preserved lemons
        & zhoug 130
    tagliatelle with herbed lentils 212
    Turkish bride soup 182
Lesvos, Greece 11–12, 91, 105, 115,
    130, 137–43, 171–8, 230, 268
lettuce cups, spicy bulgur in 155
LIFE Project 196
light meals 96–135
lima beans, smoky 112
Loxandra 122

M
mackerel sandwiches, Istanbul's
    famous 214
mains 204–47
al-Mallah, Samar 196
meatballs
    classic Turkish meatballs 240–1
    Greek tomato meatballs 244
Melissa 65–8, 269

meringue: raspberry &
    pomegranate roulade 277
mezze 96–135
mint
    halloumi & mint muffins 84
    tomato & mint dolma 81–2
    yogurt with cucumber & mint 107
Mohammad 12, 232
Moria, Greece 11, 172, 174
moussaka, my vegetable 210
mousse, chocolate, orange,
    & olive oil 274
Mozhdeh 105, 177–8
muffins, halloumi & mint 84
Muhammad 12
mushroom moussaka 210
mushrooms
    arugula, mushroom, & kefalotyri
        salad 161
    mushroom moussaka 210
mussels 223
    steamed garlic & chile mussels 223

N
Nan 137–43, 161, 209
Nicosia, Cyprus 122, 206, 258,
    283–91
nuts 31

O
oats: fragrant oats with rose
    water 55
Ohilebo, Maria 66
olive oil 29, 32
    chocolate, orange, & olive oil
        mousse 274
olives
    Cypriot potato salad 152
    Greek salad 146
    olive bread 75
    sardines in grape leaves 131
    tomato & za'atar salad 156
One Happy Family 11, 172, 230, 232
onions: grilled onion salad with
    pomegranate & sumac 160
oranges: chocolate, orange, & olive
    oil mousse 274
orzo rice 79
ouzo 220

P

paprika: herb & paprika chicken 224
parsley: lentils with preserved
    lemons & zhoug 130
pasta
  orzo rice 79
  tagliatelle with herbed lentils 212
pastries
  bougatsa 272
  sweet tahini swirls 53–4
peaches: fig & peach tart 271
pear, apricot, & rose water
    pudding 260
peppers
  Broccolini with red peppers & dill
    118
  ezme salad 166
  Greek vegetable medley 128
  spicy red pepper & walnut smash
    100
  Turkish shepherd's salad 148
Persian cucumbers
  spicy bulgur in lettuce cups 155
  Turkish shepherd's salad 148
pickled red cabbage 132
pie, spinach, herb, & feta 86
pine nuts
  tagliatelle with herbed lentils 212
  Turkish semolina halva 264
pistachio & herb sauce 217
pita bread 78
Plomari, Cyprus 43, 210
polenta: halloumi saganaki 122
pomegranate 283
  beet, fennel, & pomegranate
    salad 165
  halloumi saganaki 122
  raspberry & pomegranate
    roulade 277
  spicy bulgur in lettuce cups 155
  tagliatelle with herbed lentils 212
pomegranate molasses 31, 155
  grilled onion salad with
    pomegranate & sumac 160
  pomegranate & sumac
    chicken 230
  tagliatelle with herbed lentils
    212
pork: Greek tomato meatballs 244

potatoes 284
  Cypriot potato salad 152
  Greek vegetable medley 128
  lamb shank kleftiko 235–6
  skordalia 218
prawn saganaki 220
preserved lemons: lentils
    with lemons & zhoug 130
pul biber 30–1
  adana kebabs 237
  charred cabbage with hazelnuts
    & chile butter 126
  eggs with yogurt & chile butter 56
  hot yogurt & spinach soup 184
  pomegranate & sumac chicken 230
  spiced tomato scramble 59
  spicy red pepper & walnut smash
    100
  steamed garlic & chile mussels 223
pumpkin
  Afghan spiced pumpkin 115
  candied pumpkin with tahini &
    date syrup 266
  pumpkin & cardamom soup 190

R

raisins: veiled rice with spiced
    chicken 227–8
Rakhine chicken curry 232
raspberry & pomegranate
    roulade 277
Reem 230
rice 71
  orzo rice 79
  tomato & mint dolma 81–2
  veiled rice with spiced chicken 227–8
ricotta: honey & ricotta cake 269
Rohingya tribe 232
rose water
  fragrant oats with rose water 55
  pear, apricot, & rose water
    pudding 260
roulade, raspberry & pomegranate
    277

S

saganaki
  halloumi saganaki 122
  prawn saganaki 220

Sajaad 172
salads 144–69
  arugula, mushroom, & kefalotyri
    salad 161
  beet, fennel, & pomegranate
    salad 165
  crunchy winter slaw 162
  Cypriot potato salad 152
  ezme salad 166
  garlicky eggplant salad 99
  Greek salad 145, 146
  grilled onion salad with
    pomegranate & sumac 160
  sunshine salad 158
  sweet potato, chickpea, & tahini
    salad 151
  tomato & za'atar salad 156
  Turkish shepherd's salad 148
Samos, Greece 91
sandwiches, Istanbul's famous
    mackerel 214
sardines in grape leaves 131
sauce, yogurt 115
sea bream with pistachio
    & herb smash 217
seasonings 32
seeds 31
semolina
  halloumi saganaki 122
  Turkish semolina halva 264
serving food 32
sesame seeds 31
shallots: beef stifado 243
shepherd's salad, Turkish 148
side dishes 96–135
Sislo 11, 12
slaw, crunchy winter 162
smoked cod's roe: taramasalata
    103
smoky lima beans 112
Smyrna 244
soups 180–91
  hot yogurt & spinach soup
    184
  lemon chicken soup 189
  pumpkin & cardamom soup
    190
  spiced carrot soup 187
  Turkish bride soup 182

sour cherries
  sour cherry cheesecake 263
  sour cherry jam 50
spices 30–1
  spiced carrot soup 187
  spiced cornbread with feta 76
  spiced tomato scramble 59
  spicy bulgur in lettuce cups 155
  spicy red pepper & walnut smash 100
spinach
  ezme salad 166
  Greek greens 101
  hot yogurt & spinach soup 184
  spinach, herb, & feta pie 86
Stani café 257
Stephanos 181
stifado, beef 243
Stratis 140
sujuk & eggs 60
sumac 31
  grilled onion salad with pomegranate & sumac 160
  pomegranate & sumac chicken 230
sunshine salad 158
sweet potatoes
  sunshine salad 158
  sweet potato, chickpea, & tahini salad 151
sweet tahini swirls 53–4
Syria 171, 196, 230, 252

T
tahini 31
  candied pumpkin with tahini & date syrup 266
  grape molasses & tahini on toast 48
  sweet potato, chickpea, & tahini salad 151
  sweet tahini swirls 53–4
Talli, Mahmud 12, 230
taramasalata 103

tart, fig & peach 271
toast
  cardamom egg toast 54
  delicious things on toast 48–51
tomatoes 156
  Afghan spiced pumpkin 115
  beef stifado 243
  ezme salad 166
  Greek salad 146
  Greek tomato meatballs 244
  Greek vegetable medley 128
  mushroom moussaka 210
  prawn saganaki 220
  Rakhine chicken curry 232
  smoky lima beans 112
  spiced tomato scramble 59
  spicy bulgur in lettuce cups 155
  stuffed roasted eggplants 116
  sunshine salad 158
  tomato & mint dolma 81–2
  tomato & za'atar salad 156
  Turkish shepherd's salad 148
Turkey 22, 140
  breakfasts 43
  Cyprus 27, 283, 284–7, 288–91
  hazelnuts 126
  pantry ingredients 29–31
  soups 181
  vegetables 145
Turkish braised carrots & leeks 121
Turkish bride soup 182
Turkish flatbread 72
Turkish meatballs 240–1
Turkish semolina halva 264
Turkish shepherd's salad 148
Turkish white beans 108
turnips: crunchy winter slaw 162

U
United Nations 177, 284–7
  Green Line buffer zone 27, 258, 287, 291

V
vegetables 145
  Greek vegetable medley 128

mushroom moussaka 210
  see also individual types of vegetable
veiled rice with spiced chicken 227–8

W
Waida 140
walnuts
  date & walnut brownies 278
  Iranian eggplant & kashk dip 105–6
  kaymak, honey, & walnuts on toast 48
  spicy red pepper & walnut smash 100
white beans, Turkish 108
winter slaw, crunchy 162

Y
Yalkın, Çizge 81, 288
yellow split mung beans: almost fava 110
Yemen 130, 196
yogurt 29–30
  eggs with yogurt & chile butter 56
  garlicky eggplant salad 99
  griddled fruits, yogurt, & honey 46
  halloumi & mint muffins 84
  hot yogurt & spinach soup 184
  raspberry & pomegranate roulade 277
  sour cherry cheesecake 263
  spiced cornbread with feta 76
  yogurt drink 106
  yogurt sauce 115
  yogurt with cucumber & mint 107

Z
za'atar: tomato & za'atar salad 156
zhoug, lentils with preserved lemons & 130
zucchini & feta fritters 125

First American Edition 2021

Originally published in Great Britain under the title *Ripe Figs: Recipes and Stories from the Eastern Mediterranean*

Printed in the United States of America

For information about permission to reproduce selections from this book, write to Permissions, W. W. Norton & Company, Inc., 500 Fifth Avenue, New York, NY 10110

For information about special discounts for bulk purchases, please contact W. W. Norton Special Sales at specialsales@wwnorton.com or 800-233-4830

Manufacturing by Versa Press

ISBN 978-1-324-00665-7

W. W. Norton & Company, Inc., 500 Fifth Avenue, New York, N.Y. 10110

www.wwnorton.com

W. W. Norton & Company Ltd., 15 Carlisle Street, London W1D 3BS

2 3 4 5 6 7 8 9 0

Acknowledgments

As ever, I want to thank everyone who took the time to meet with me and eat with me, especially those who welcomed a stranger (and a photographer) into their homes. My travels for my books always remind me that the world isn't such a bad place after all, and the generosity and openness of the human spirit—especially in the Eastern Mediterranean and the Middle East—is something that often fills me with hope for our planet's future.

Thanks to my agent Clare Hulton and the brilliant team at Bloomsbury who always work so hard to bring my books together, give me the space to write about the issues I care about, and make them look as beautiful as they do. Thank you Richard Atkinson, Natalie Bellos, Rowan Yapp, Lucy Bannell, Kitty Stogdon, Donough Shanahan, Ellen Williams, Maud Davies, and Laura Brodie. I am always grateful for the support you give me and the expertise you bring with you. Thanks also to Melanie Tortoroli and Will Scarlett from W. W. Norton who gave me the confidence to take the book in the direction it ended up in, and to Smith & Gilmour for their innovation and creativity in designing this gorgeous book.

Thanks to Matt Russell for his photography, Rosie Reynolds and Jen Kay for making the food look so delicious, and to Catherine Phipps for helping me to perfect the recipes. I feel very lucky to have you all on my team.

Thanks to Loizos Kapsalis and Gonca Karakök for being such wonderful guides, and to Julia Mills, who caught me in Istanbul just when I needed it.

Thanks to Mum, Dad, Maryam, Chris, Kasia, Natascha, Dave, and Lucy for always having faith and helping me to persevere with this book when times got tough. And to Glynn and Stephanos, for yet again reflecting an idea for a book back to me and encouraging me to go for it.

And finally, thanks to Julian, without whom this book never would have been conceived, whose influence is woven through almost every page, and who polished off more meals than was necessary in order to perfect the recipes. Thanks for helping me fall deeper in love with the Eastern Mediterranean.

Organizations to support

In the process of researching and writing this book, I developed a huge amount
of respect for the work of the following charities and NGOs. If you are interested
in learning more about their work, or donating to them, I urge you to do so.

Lesvos Solidarity
www.lesvossolidarity.org
A grassroots civil society network of international volunteers
supporting refugees on the Greek island of Lesvos.

One Happy Family
www.ohf-lesvos.org
A vibrant community center run jointly by international
volunteers and refugees on the Greek island of Lesvos.

Home for All
www.homeforall.eu
An NGO and charity that provides meals and essential goods
to refugees on the Greek island of Lesvos.

Melissa
www.melissanetwork.org
A network for migrant and refugee women in Greece, promoting
empowerment, communication, and active citizenship.

Help Refugees
www.helprefugees.org
A British charity supporting a wide range of refugee projects
across Europe.

Doctors Without Borders
www.doctorswithoutborders.org
An international medical humanitarian organization doing
vital work supporting refugees in the Eastern Mediterranean,
including running life-saving search and rescue operations
in the Mediterranean Sea.

About the author

Yasmin Khan is an author and broadcaster who is passionate about
sharing people's stories through food. Her critically acclaimed cookbooks,
The Saffron Tales and *Zaitoun*, chronicle her culinary adventures through Iran
and Palestine, sharing recipes and stories that celebrate beauty and the
power of the human spirit in regions more commonly associated with conflict.
Before working in food, Yasmin was a human rights campaigner for a decade,
with a special focus on the Middle East. *Ripe Figs* is her third book.

www.yasminkhanstories.com

 yasmin_khan

 yasminkhanstories